WHAT THE
SAINTS SAID
ABOUT HEAVEN

WHAT THE SAINTS SAID ABOUT HEAVEN

101 Holy Insights about Everlasting Life

**Ronda Chervin, PhD,
Richard Ballard, DMin,
and Ruth Ballard, MDiv**

TAN Books
Charlotte, North Carolina

ISBN: 978-0-89555-872-5

Cover design by Milo Persic, milo.persic@gmail.com.

Cover image: Detail of Heaven from the Last Judgment, Angelico, Fra (Guido di Pietro) (c.1387–1455) / Museo di San Marco dell'Angelico, Florence, Italy / The Bridgeman Art Library International

Icons © Ruth Ballard. All rights reserved.

All quotations from the Catechism (CCC) are taken from the *Catechism of the Catholic Church* (second edition). Doubleday, 2003

All Scripture quotations are taken from the Catholic Edition of the Revised Standard Version of the Bible, copyright 1965, 1966 National Council of the Churches of Christ in the United States of America.

Some Saints' quotations have been abridged for length or clarity.

Printed and Bound in the United States of America.

TAN Books
Charlotte, North Carolina
2011

Prayer to St. Joseph, patron of a happy death:
O Blessed Joseph,
who yielded up your last breath
in the arms of Jesus and Mary,
obtain for me this grace,
O holy Joseph,
that I may breathe forth my soul in praise,
saying in spirit,
if I am unable to do so in words:
"Jesus, Mary and Joseph,
I give you my heart and my soul."
Amen

Ruth's dedication:
To Richard, my husband and best friend, for his ever-constant love and support; to Ruth M. Carpenter, my grandmother, for her example of faith and courage both in life and in death; to Jody Cole, my teacher and friend, who shared her passion for iconography and the profound spirituality of this sacred craft; and to all my friends and family who have been with me on the journey

Richard's dedication:
To my dear wife Ruth, who in our marriage has taught me the meaning of "the spousal love of Christ and the Church": much love and gratitude as we journey on our way to eternal life

Ronda's dedication:
For Charles Rich, RIP, who introduced me to reading the Catholic mystics

Contents

Illustrations

St. Joseph the Betrothed, St. Joseph the Provider. Prototype, probably 20th century, based on a detail from an ancient icon, The Presentation, c. 1500, Russia. The modern prototype is by an unknown artist.

The Old Testament Trinity. Prototype, Andrei Rublev, c. 1411, Russia. The persons of the Triune God are portrayed as angelic beings. Rublev probably based his icon upon the prototype of St. Sergius of Radonezh's "Icon of The Hospitality of Abraham," late 14th century. The icon depicted here was adapted from a pattern based on the ancient prototype as developed by iconographer Jody Cole, and was used by permission of the artist in the creation of the icon.

The Marriage Embrace of St Joachim and St. Anne, The Conception of the Virgin. Prototype, Russian, 15th century. Saints Joachim and Anne are joined together as one in an intimate, loving embrace as husband and wife. The pattern is an original composition by the author.

Our Lady of Korsun, The Virgin of the Sweet Kiss. This particular prototype originates in Italy, 19th century. Icons of this type were popular from the 5th century onward, throughout Russia, the Balkans, and Italy. Tradition holds that St. Luke himself wrote the very first prototype of this icon. In this icon, Mary, depicted in half-figure, embraces her son in an intensely loving, warm caress, with faces touching cheek to cheek. The icon depicted here was adapted from a pattern based on the ancient prototype as developed by iconographer Jody Cole, and was used by permission of the artist in the creation of the icon.

Fish Mosaic Icon, based on a detail from the Creation Dome, San Marco, Venice, Italy, 13th century: "Creation of the birds and marine creatures." The mosaic is a composition by the author.

Icon of the Resurrection **84**
The Harrowing of Hell, Anastasis. Prototype, late 13th century, Mt
Sinai. The resurrected Christ tramples the gates of Hell, and through
his sacrifice on the cross, rescues humanity, represented by Adam
and Eve, from sin, death, and the devil. The icon depicted here was
adapted from a pattern based on the ancient prototype as developed
by iconographer Jody Cole, and was used by permission of the artist
in the creation of the icon. The image of the demon/devil used in the
Icon of the Resurrection was adapted from an image originally drawn
by Bro. Martin Erspamer, OSB (formerly Steve Erspamer), and is used
by permission of the artist.

Icon of St. Veronica **106**
Prototype, in the style of the Western Tradition, 20th century. St. Veronica holds the holy face (Mandylion, "not made by human hands")
that was imprinted miraculously by Christ upon her veil. The holy
face is based upon an ancient prototype. The pattern is an original
composition by the author.

Icon of the Cleansing of the Temple **116**
Prototype, original, 21st century. Jesus is depicted according to the
Biblical account of St. John 2:12- 25. The pattern is an original com-
position by the author.

Preface

Ronda Chervin

A year or so ago, I was visiting my dear friends Ruth and Richard Ballard in their beautiful home in South Carolina. They are both gourmet cooks. Since I am an old woman in her seventies and they are younger but post–middle age, it is not so surprising that our talk touched on a question of burning interest: will we eat in Heaven?

You may think there is a simple answer: since Jesus spoke about eating and drinking in Heaven, it must be so. But none other than St. Thomas Aquinas taught that this would be some kind of spiritualized repast in order to avoid, among other things, messy digestive processes in Heaven!

As we pursued the issue, the subject broadened to include many other controversial topics, and somehow it all evolved into this outcome: wouldn't it be wonderful to assemble a book of what the Saints had to say about Heaven? It was but a hop, skip, and a jump to thinking it would be even better to include what they've said about preparing for Heaven.

The division of labor developed quite naturally. All three of us would go on a treasure hunt, with the help of trusty Brother Web, for quotations. I would write a prayer for each quotation; Richard would write the introductions; and Ruth would "write," as they say, the icons. And so was born the book you hold in your hands.

"Blessed be the pure of heart, for they shall see God."[1] I think of these beautiful lines from the Beatitudes as referring not only to the pure of heart's seeing God in Heaven but to their wisdom while still on earth. I think that since they are pure in heart, the beatified and canonized holy ones have greater insight than the rest of us, no matter what our own wisdom or aspirations to holiness. I think this is true even though the Saints have been canonized not for their writings but for their heroic virtues and their miracles. And so even though these quotations should not be considered infallible, their sources make them worthy of deep and serious reflection.

In doing the research and writing the contemporary prayers to match, I found that I was enlightened, reassured, and fired up to try harder to prepare for so wonderful a destiny. I hope you will feel the same way.

Our Lady, Seat of Wisdom, pray for us.

---

1 *Matt.* 5:8

Introduction

Deacon Richard Ballard

Although I have had the good fortune to travel to a number of different countries around the world, there are still a great many places that I would like to be able to visit. I would like to visit Africa and go on a safari. I would like to go to Hawaii and witness the lava flow from Kilauea, one of the world's most active volcanoes. I have been to Rome several times, but I also would like to explore the cities and towns around the rest of Italy. I would like to visit Mount Athos in Greece and see the numerous ancient icons, relics, texts, art objects, and other irreplaceable riches that are to be found on the Holy Mountain. I would like to go to Axum, Ethiopia, to the Church of Our Lady Mary of Zion, where they claim to have the original Ark of the Covenant; and I would like to make a pilgrimage to Saint Catherine's Monastery at the foot of Mount Sinai in Egypt, where tradition has it that God appeared to Moses in the burning bush.

All these places, and many more, are on my prospective itinerary of sites to visit, and I hope one day to be able to travel to all of them. In the meantime, however, I can still gain a sense of what these places and their people and treasures are like by becoming an armchair traveler. I can experience their sights and sounds by reading about them from the written perspectives of knowledgeable guides and reliable experts who are familiar with their aspects and nuances. Through their guidance

I can not only experience a little of these places—I can prepare myself for someday visiting them in person.

In similar fashion, this book is a guide to a place that we hope one day not just to visit but to remain in. Our guides and experts are the Saints and the authoritative teachings of the Church.

The glossary of the *Catechism of the Catholic Church* tells us that a Saint is a "holy one who leads a life in union with God through the grace of Christ and receives the reward of eternal life." Since the Saints, "being more closely united to Christ"[1] have already merited eternal life with God in Heaven, we do well to consult and make use of their unique understanding regarding the nature of Heaven and how we should prepare ourselves to go there. Likewise, the Catholic Church is the "pillar and foundation of the truth,"[2] which authoritatively, authentically, and infallibly provides us with the means of sanctification to be able to reach this goal—for the Church itself is the "universal sacrament of salvation."[3]

May this little travel guide from the Saints be your companion along the way to Heaven: a descriptive narrative of what Heaven is like but, most importantly, a manual of how to get there. May all of us, relying upon the mercy of God and the intercession of all the Saints, achieve that end.

---

1 *CCC*, 956.
2 *CCC*, 171.
3 *CCC*, 849.

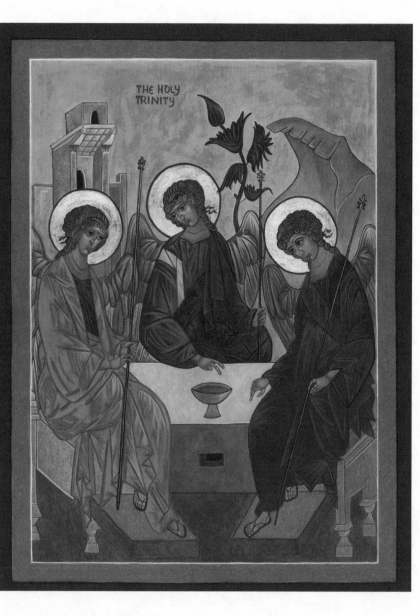

I

In Heaven, We Will Be United with God

Typically, when we try to speak about what Heaven will be like, we begin by saying that its most essential attribute is being with God. Of course, we are quick to add that Heaven will also include the experience of being with the Angels and Saints, the experience of seeing our departed loved ones again, and many other wonderful characteristics as well. Even so, we always come back to the basic premise that the fundamental quality of Heaven is being in the presence of God. And in the presence of God, we will see Him as He is (*1 Jn.* 3:2); we will rejoice with exquisite happiness in the reward of that vision (*Matt.* 5:12); we will be at perfect peace (*Eph.* 2:14); and we will be loved by Him and in return will love Him and others fully and completely, for He is perfect love (*1 Jn.* 4:7–11). This glorious experience of the Saints in light is called the Beatific Vision. The *Catechism of the Catholic Church* tells us, "Because of his transcendence, God cannot be seen as he is, unless he himself opens up his mystery to man's immediate contemplation and gives him the capacity for it. The Church calls this contemplation of God in his heavenly glory 'the Beatific Vision.'"[1]

---

1 *Catechism of the Catholic Church* (second edition). Doubleday, 2003, 1028, p. 290.

As a gift of His own self-revelation, the redeemed souls in Heaven will enjoy a direct, unmediated perception of the Holy Trinity, the God who "dwells in unapproachable light" (*1 Tim.* 6:16). They will have immediate access to His presence and will see Him "face to face" (*1 Cor.* 13:12). In doing so, as St. Thomas Aquinas asserts, they will "enjoy the same happiness wherewith God is happy, seeing Him in the way which He sees Himself."[2] This experience will be an eternal, infinite, and unbounded source of perfect and inestimable fulfillment. As the *Catechism* states, "The Beatific Vision, in which God opens himself in an inexhaustible way to the elect, will be the ever-flowing well-spring of happiness, peace, and mutual communion."[3]

For the redeemed, this will be the completion of their vocation to eternal life, the calling and gift they originally received in Baptism with the infusion of sanctifying grace. It will be the culmination of the work of their sanctification that the Holy Spirit began when they became the adopted children of God through baptismal regeneration. It will be the realization of the ultimate end for which they were created. This intimate familiarity of the redeemed with their Creator, this union with Almighty God, will have a profound impact on these souls. They will be transformed into His very likeness (*2 Cor.* 3:18), and the glory of this transformation, this union with God, will result in their sharing in His Divinity!

For many, this last statement may seem shocking. Mere human beings sharing in the Divinity of the Godhead? Unthinkable! And yet this is the destiny of all the redeemed. As St. Peter

---

2   *Of God and His Creatures: An Annotated Translation of the* Summa Contra Gentiles *of Saint Thomas Aquinas,* Joseph Rickaby, S.J., London: Burns and Oates, 1905, 225.

3   *CCC,* 1045, p. 295.

wrote, "His divine power has granted to us all things that pertain to life and godliness, through the knowledge of him who called us to his own glory and excellence, by which he has granted to us his precious and very great promises, that through these you may escape from the corruption that is in the world because of passion, and become partakers of the divine nature" (*2 Peter* 1:3–4).

This, in fact, was the purpose of the Incarnation of Our Lord: that our salvation and sanctification might be so perfectly accomplished and realized that we could thereby share in His divine nature. The *Catechism*, quoting St. Peter, St. Irenaeus, St. Athanasius, and St. Thomas Aquinas, puts it this way: "The Word became flesh to make us '*partakers of the divine nature*': 'For this is why the Word became man, and the Son of God became the Son of man: so that man, by entering into communion with the Word and thus receiving divine sonship, might become a son of God.' 'For the Son of God became man so that we might become God.' 'The only-begotten Son of God, wanting to make us sharers in his divinity, assumed our nature, so that he, made man, might make men gods.'"[4] What does it mean that by sharing in His Divinity we might be made gods? First of all, it must be said that there is only one, eternal God—Father, Son, and Holy Spirit—the Holy Trinity; there are no others. The second person of the Holy Trinity, the Son, who was begotten eternally of the Father, took on human flesh in the womb of the Blessed Virgin Mary at the time of the Incarnation. At that moment, He became truly human as well as truly Divine, the God-man, Jesus Christ. As confessed in the Athanasian Creed,

> For the right faith is that we believe and confess that our Lord Jesus Christ, the Son of God, is God and man. God

---

4   *CCC*, 460, p. 128.

of the substance of the Father, begotten before the worlds; and man of substance of His mother, born in the world. Perfect God and perfect man, of a reasonable soul and human flesh subsisting. Equal to the Father as touching His Godhead, and inferior to the Father as touching His manhood. Who, although He is God and man, yet He is not two, but one Christ. One, not by conversion of the Godhead into flesh, but by taking of that manhood into God. One altogether, not by confusion of substance, but by unity of person.[5]

Jesus Christ is God by nature; that we can never be. We will never become divine as the Holy Trinity is divine. We will never achieve ontological equality with God. We will always have a human nature and will not assume a divine one. However, because of the saving work Our Lord accomplished, we can become "gods" by analogy through the grace of adoption as the Father's children. This is realized through the infusion of sanctifying grace into our souls. So to state that we become "gods" is simply an analogous way of saying that, as the adopted sons and daughters of God, the culmination of our sanctification in Heaven—our perfection in holiness—results in our sharing in His Divinity. We become like God to such an extent that we participate in His Divine nature. In Western theology this is called divinization or deification, while the churches of the East refer to it as *theosis.*

What a magnificent hope to contemplate! Who can say fully what sharing in the divinity of God will mean? What wonders beyond comprehension must await the righteous souls who persevere to the end and receive the unfading crown of

5 www.thecatholictreasurechest.com/creeds.htm

glory? Truly, no "eye has seen, nor ear heard, nor the heart of man conceived, what God has prepared for those who love him" (*1 Cor.* 2:9).

Day 1

Every eye will see Him.   *—Rev.* 1:7

We have received, as John has told us, an anointing by the Holy One which teaches us inwardly more than our tongue can speak. Let us turn to this source of knowledge, and because at present you cannot see, make it your business to desire the divine vision. The entire life of a good Christian is in fact an exercise of holy desire. You do not yet see what you long for, but the very act of desiring prepares you, so that when he comes you may see and be utterly satisfied.   —St. Augustine

O St. John and St. Augustine, your minds and hearts burned with desire to see God. Some of us, thinking that Heaven is too good to be true, fail to make it our "business to desire the divine vision." Instead we burn with desire for happiness, or at least a diminishment of suffering, on earth. As we begin our reading about what the Saints said about Heaven, may the Holy Spirit fill us with desire to one day reach Heaven, through Christ Our Lord. Amen.

Day 2

Then Jesus came from Galilee to the Jordan to John, to be baptized by him. . . . And when Jesus was baptized, he went up immediately from the water, and behold, the heavens were opened and he saw the Spirit of God descending like a dove and alighting on him; and lo, a voice from heaven, saying, "This is my beloved Son, with whom I am well pleased."   —Matt. 3:13–17

Today let us do honor to Christ's baptism and celebrate this feast in holiness. Be cleansed entirely and continue to be cleansed. Nothing gives such pleasure to God as the conversion and salvation of men, for whom his every word and every revelation exist. He wants you to become a living force for all mankind, lights shining in the world. You are to be radiant lights as you stand beside Christ, the great light, bathed in the glory of him who is the light of heaven. You are to enjoy more and more the pure and dazzling light of the Trinity, as now you have received—though not in its fullness—a ray of its splendor, proceeding from the one God, in Christ Jesus our Lord, to whom be glory and power forever and ever. Amen.   —St. Gregory Nazianzen

Holy Trinity, our mysterious God. We long to see that "dazzling light" that St. Gregory wrote about. In our lives on earth, how welcome is the light of dawn after a long dark night. How dazzling is the light of the sun's rays on the ocean waves. Through Your grace, bring us out of the darkness of our ignorance into the dazzling light of Your Supreme Being. Amen.

Day 3

Blessed are the poor in heart, for they shall see God.

—Matt. 5:8

All the blessed in heaven, though they may have been while on earth simple and ignorant, are now possessed of the deepest wisdom, and so endowed with the virtue of justice, that they might justly become kings of any kingdom. For all the blessed behold the very essence of God Himself, and thereby, from this fountain of uncreated wisdom, they drink in such wisdom as neither Solomon nor any other mortal possessed, except our Lord Jesus Christ, who, even during the time of His mortal life, saw God, for in Him "were hid all the treasures of wisdom and knowledge."

—St. Robert Bellarmine

O Holy Spirit, in our culture we put education on a pedestal, though little we learn in school is about the great truths regarding our Creator, our Redeemer, or You, the Holy Spirit. We ask You to take away from our minds all the false ideas that have come to us from bad teaching or from the media. We ask You to pull together for us everything we have ever learned that is true about nature, human beings, and, most of all, about the Trinity. With our minds longing for the whole truth, we open ourselves to Your inspirations as You lead us to the eternal Truth. Amen.

Day 4

And suddenly there was with the angel a multitude of the heavenly host praising God and singing, "Glory to God in the highest."　　　　　　　　　　　　　　　　　　*—Luke 2:13–14*

When during adoration, I repeated the prayer, 'Holy God' several times, a vivid presence of God suddenly swept over me, and I was caught up in spirit before the majesty of God. I saw how the Angels and the Saints of the Lord give glory to God. The glory of God is so great that I dare not try to describe it, because I would not be able to do so, and souls might think that what I have written is all there is. Saint Paul, I understand now why you did not want to describe heaven, but only said that eye has not seen, nor ear heard, nor has it entered into the heart of man what God has prepared for those who love him. Now I have seen the way in which I adore God; oh how miserable it is! And what a tiny drop it is in comparison to that perfect heavenly glory.　　—St. Faustina

Dear Holy Family, you were present at the birth of that baby whose coming the shepherds heard the Angels singing about. St. Luke's account has inspired countless artists to try to depict the glory found in a small infant. A glimpse of the glory of the Father Himself was given to many Saints and mystics. We beg You to show us, Your faithful flock, such a glimpse to help us on our journey through this valley of tears. Amen.

Day 5

Rejoice in the Lord, always, again, I will say rejoice.
—*Phil.* 4:4

That [when we see God] will be the great joy, the supreme joy, joy in all its fullness. Then we shall no longer drink the milk of hope, but we shall feed on the reality itself. Nevertheless, even now, before that vision comes to us, or before we come to that vision, let us rejoice in the Lord for it is no small reason for rejoicing to have a hope that will someday be fulfilled.   —St. Augustine

Holy Spirit, "refreshment in the noonday heat," as You are called in the famous hymn, "Veni, Sancte Spiritus," how is it that we who have hope of heavenly bliss rejoice so little now? We think of the joy of a champion sportsman about to enter the arena where he expects to triumph, or of the joy of a mother feeling the first kick of the baby in her womb, or of engaged couples dreaming of the union they will have on their wedding day. But we Christians, with so much greater a hope, let our spirits be dragged down by the devil into a state of fear, dullness, and discouragement. Rouse our hearts in praise so that all may see the joy we have in our hope. Amen.

Day 6

[Thomas] said, "Unless I see in his hands the print of the nails, and place my finger in the mark of the nails, and place my hand in his side, I will not believe." Eight days later . . . Jesus came and stood among them, and . . . said to Thomas, "Put your finger here, and see my hands and put out your hand and place it in my side; do not be faithless, but believing." Thomas answered him, "My Lord and my God!" —John 20:24–28

I told you of the happiness which the glorified body would take in the glorified humanity of My only-begotten Son, which gives you assurance of your resurrection. There, they exult in His wounds, which have remained fresh, and the scars in His Body are preserved, and continually cry for mercy for you, to Me, the Supreme and Eternal Father. And they are all conformed with Him, in joyousness and mirth, and you will all be conformed with Him, eye with eye, and hand with hand, and with the whole Body of the sweet Word My Son, and, dwelling in Me, you will dwell in Him, because He is one thing with Me. But their bodily eye, as I told you, will delight itself in the glorified humanity of the Word, My only-begotten Son. Why so? Because their life finished in the affection of My love, and therefore will this delight endure for them eternally. —St. Catherine of Siena

Dear St. Catherine, we believe that God the Father spoke these words in your heart for our enlightenment. Visions such as these can help us think of Heaven. Some of us must blush to say that we fear Heaven will be boring. Just imagine our excitement to one day see Your wounds, beloved Jesus, and even touch them. Amen.

Day 7

"What no eye has seen, nor ear heard, nor the heart of man conceived, what God has prepared for those who love him," God has revealed to us through the Spirit.   —*1 Cor. 2:9–10*

In heaven all the senses are evermore, and without fear of loss, fully satisfied with their pleasures, and drowned in the depth of unspeakable delight. In the sight of God we shall have the fullness of felicity, which neither eye hath seen, nor ear heard, nor man's heart conceived. The understanding shall be without error, the memory without forgetfulness, the will without evil desires. The thoughts pure and comfortable, the affections subordinate and measurable, all the passions governed by reason, and settled by perfect calm. No fear shall affright us, no presumption puff us up, no love disquiet us, no anger incense us, no envy gnaw us, no pusillanimity quail us, but courage, constancy, charity, peace, and security shall replenish and establish our hearts, not only shall we love, but be also loved.   —St. Robert Southwell

Jesus, we read St. Robert's list of our miseries and we shudder. Are we not made wretched by our numerous vices, faults, and defects every day of our lives on earth? And not only our own, but also those of others who victimize us in small and, sometimes, in very great ways each day! And yet how we cling to whatever we now have, often more afraid of an unpredictable death than of these very predictable woes! Help us, O Lord; help us, please, to let Your present love for us flood our hearts so that we may be filled with grace and virtue and so that even when the cross is heavy we may have peace and hope. Amen.

Day 8

But about midnight Paul and Silas were praying and singing hymns to God, and the prisoners were listening to them.

—*Acts* 16:25

It is not said, "May the joy of thy Lord enter into thee," but "Enter thou into the joy of thy Lord," which is a proof that the joy will be greater than we can conceive. We shall enter into a great sea of divine and eternal joy, which will fill us within and without, and surround us on all sides.   —St. Robert Bellarmine

Holy Spirit, in our times we speak so often of going within to find God. Many of us need, precisely, to stop looking around for God and instead go within in silence to find Him. At the same time, the Church teaches us the need to also tap into the power of joy that comes from going out of ourselves in spoken praise. Can you show each of us what form of praise will help us most to enter into the joy of the Lord now as a foretaste of Heaven? In Heaven, as St. Robert understood, we will experience joy in God both within and without. Alleluia. Amen.

Day 9

No sound is heard of weeping
For pain and sorrow cease
And sin shall reign no longer
But love and joy and peace.

—*Liturgy of the Hours*,
"Hymn for Common of
Holy Women," Morning Prayer

Take all the pleasures of all the spheres, and multiply each
through endless years. One minute of heaven is worth them all.
—St. Thomas More

Father God, You have filled the world with pleasurable things for us to enjoy even as we struggle with heavy crosses. Let us think of some of those pleasures we enjoy, such as the beauty of the ocean, the delicious taste of ice cream, or the sight of a baby's first smile. When St. Thomas More wrote these lines about Heaven, he was living in a prison awaiting martyrdom by the axe! So right now, no matter what the pain we are feeling, help us to lift up our minds to the thought of our favorite pleasures and then think that when we are in Heaven our pains will seem tiny in comparison to our joys. Amen.

Day 10

To him who conquers I will give some of the hidden manna.
                                                        —*Rev.* 2:17

*And yet, whereas such be the joys of heaven that are prepared
for every saved soul, our Lord says yet, by the mouth of St. John,
that he will give his holy martyrs who suffer for his sake many a
special kind of joy. For he says, "To him that overcomes, I shall give
him to eat of the tree of life. And I shall confess his name before my
Father and before his angels." And also he says, "Fear none of those
things that you shall suffer . . . but be faithful unto the death, and
I shall give thee the crown of life. He that overcomes shall not be
hurt of the second death." And he says also, "To him that conquers
will I give manna secret and hid." If we wished to enlarge upon
this, and were able to declare these special gifts, with yet others
then would it appear how far those heavenly joys shall surmount
above all the comfort that ever came in the mind of any man living
here upon earth.*   —St. Thomas More

St. Thomas More, when you wrote of conquering fear,
you were trying to encourage Catholics to risk martyrdom in
defense of the Faith. In our times, even if we are not called to risk
our lives, we still have to conquer other fears. How fearful we can
be of painful, disabling illness; of the effects of economic reces-
sion; or of abandonment by those dear to us. St. Thomas More,
please intercede for us that faith in Christ's promise of heavenly
"manna" can keep us from succumbing to such fears. Amen.

Day 11

Blessed are those who dwell in Thy house, ever singing Thy praise.   —*Ps.* 84:4

To dwell in the house of the good God, to enjoy the presence of the good God, to be happy with the happiness of the good God—oh, what happiness, my children! Who can understand all the joy and consolation with which the saints are inebriated in Paradise? St. Paul, who was taken up into the third heaven, tells us that there are things above which he cannot reveal to us, and which we cannot comprehend. Indeed, my children, we can never form a true idea of Heaven till we shall be there. It is a hidden treasure, an abundance of secret sweetness, a plenitude of joy, which may be felt, but which our poor tongue cannot explain. What can we imagine greater? The good God Himself will be our recompense. O God! The happiness you promise us is such that the eyes of man cannot see it, his ears cannot hear it, nor his heart conceive it. Rejoice! for you possess all good things in one—the source of all good, the good God Himself.   —St. John Vianney

St. John Vianney, we might become perplexed in reading your beautiful words. If, indeed, it is impossible to describe the wonderful joys of Heaven, maybe we would be better off not talking or writing about it at all! But when we read your words, St. John Vianney, we might also think that if you, a Saint, could write so eloquently about Heaven, it must be because you experienced overwhelming foretastes of Heaven while still on earth. We are afraid to beg for such experiences, fearing it would make us proud. We come to you, St. John, alive now in the Heaven you savored so sweetly before your death. Intercede for us that we may open our hearts to receive more foretastes of the joy of Heaven and not become proud, but be able better to resist the temptation to melancholy and despair. Amen.

Day 12

"There was a rich man . . . and at his gate lay a poor man named Lazarus, full of sores . . . the dogs came and licked his sores. The poor man died and was carried by the angels to Abraham's bosom."   —*Luke* 16:19–22

Your reward in heaven will make up completely for all your pain and suffering.   —St. John Bosco

Jesus, compassionate one! How loving was Your heart that felt such tenderness for the beggar in Your parable. Few of us have fallen so low that dogs come to lick our sores, but all of us have felt that humbled at some time in our lives. You want us to picture our own poor selves being carried by Angels to Your bosom! In Heaven Your lavish love will heal all the painful sores of our lives. You tell us through your Saint, John Bosco, that when we feel as if we are lying on the ground with no strength to go on, we are to lift our heads up from the place where we are lying to seek our reward. Give us the same wondering hope of those who first heard this story from Your lips. Amen.

Day 13

The saints find their home in the kingdom of heaven; their life is eternal peace.   —*Liturgy of the Hours,* "Canticle of Mary," Evening Antiphon for the Common of One Martyr

All things belong to God, who supplies all with a suitable dwelling place, even as his Word says that a share is allotted to all by the Father, according as each person is or shall be worthy. And this is the couch on which the guests shall recline, having been invited to the wedding.   —St. Irenaeus

St. Irenaeus, Doctor of the Church, thank you for this cozy image of Heaven—reclining on a couch! You understood that it is impossible for human beings, made up of a combination of soul and body, to think of our heavenly reward only in terms of spiritual realities. Rest is a state we think of most in connection with our bodies and then, by analogy, with our hearts. But how we long for rest in our peaceless, often frantically paced world! Intercede for us, St. Irenaeus, that one day we will join you in perfect peace in Heaven. Amen.

Day 14

And the peace of God, which passes all understanding, will keep your hearts and your minds in Christ Jesus.   —Phil. 4:7

The Father's purpose in revealing the Son was to make Himself known to us all and so to welcome into eternal rest those who believe in him, establishing them in justice, preserving them from death.   —St. Irenaeus

God, the Father, when we think of peace, we often think simply of an absence: an absence of war, an absence of trouble, an absence of frustration, or an absence of worry. But the peace that passes all understanding, giving true rest, comes from closeness to God. When, after great separate trials, a husband and wife clasp each other in a close embrace, they cannot at that moment feel all those peaceless emotions; all they feel is the security and safety of love. If we can sometimes do this for each other, how much more can You, our God, hold us in so close an embrace that we can be at peace? Amen.

Day 15

"Father, I desire that they also, whom Thou has given me, may be with me where I am."   *—John* 17:24

You have made us for yourself, O God, and our hearts are restless until they rest in you.   —St. Augustine

O Holy Spirit, surely You inspired these famous words of St. Augustine. That our hearts are restless, we well know. What we know less is that You truly have made us for Yourself, O God. You tell us in Genesis that the animals are gifts to us. In a like manner, You have created us as gifts for Yourself. As we teach cats and dogs to be fit to live in our homes, teach us, God, to live in Your home: Heaven. How peacefully lies a restless cat or dog in the arms of its master! Give us Your peace, even now. Amen.

Day 16

"Come to me, all who labor and are heavy-laden, and I will give you rest."   —*Matt.* 11:28

I confess that I am bewildered and lose myself at the thought of the divine goodness, a sea without shore and fathomless, of God who calls me to an eternal rest after such short and tiny labors— summons and calls me to Heaven, to that supreme good that I sought so negligently, and promises me the fruit of those tears that I sowed so sparingly.   —St. Aloysius Gonzaga

O Jesus, some of us are astonished to read these words. "Short and tiny labors"! We think of our work for the Kingdom as long and huge, since we perform it with such reluctance. "Fruit of tears shed sparingly"? Many of us have never shed tears for the Kingdom, yet we long for the peace of eternal rest as if we were entitled to it. At such confessions of weakness, we glimpse a merciful smile on Your dear face, Lord. You seem to want to tell us that You love us weaklings as much as You do the Saints. Even if our labors are defective and our eyes dry of tears, You long to give us eternal rest. Help us to long for Purgatory to be purified and never to give up in our fatigue. Amen.

Day 17

"If a man loves me, he will keep my word, and my Father will love him, and we will come to him and make our home with him."   *—John 14:23*

Our home is Heaven. On earth we're like travelers staying at a hotel. When you're away, you're always thinking of going home.
                                                —St. John Vianney

Thank you, dear Jesus, for Your promise to those of us who try to follow You that You will make Your home with us. We usually think of those words as signifying the way You come within us in Holy Communion. But we can also think "home" refers to Your making a home with us in Heaven. How we exiles love to think of Heaven as our home! Lord, when we feel most uncomfortable in this world, please remind us of our heavenly home with You. Amen.

Day 18

May the souls of the faithful departed rest in peace.
—From the "Mass for the Dead"

After the fever of life—after wearinesses, sicknesses, fightings and despondings, languor and fretfulness, struggling and failing, struggling and succeeding—after all the changes and chances of this troubled and unhealthy state, at length comes death—at length the white throne of God—at length the Beatific Vision.
—Bl. John Henry Cardinal Newman

Blessed Cardinal Newman, living to such an old age with such a long life full of conflict and disappointment, this passage of yours is so moving! Sometimes we imagine that holiness is a bright, shining path up a mountain. Real Saints, we surmise, are never weary, despondent, or fretful. They would never feel anxious, even in the victory of successes, the way we often do. God, our Father in Heaven, You know every mood, every setback that each of your Saints endured. Help us to come to simple faith and trust that our rocky emotions will one day conclude. Help us to look forward to Your Heaven where we will know a steady state of peaceful bliss. Amen.

Day 19

"You did not choose me, but I chose you."   —*John* 15:16

Friendship with God brings the gift of immortality to those who accept it. In the beginning God created Adam, not because he needed man, but because he wanted to have someone on whom to bestow his blessings, He gives his life and immortality and eternal glory to those who follow and serve him, in return for their loyalty. As he said, I wish that where I am they also may be, that they may see my glory.   —St. Irenaeus

O Father God, You are so amazing. We think that because You are perfect You could not have wanted to create beings inferior to You. That is because we don't understand the logic of love. When we make things it is often not for the sake of the thing made but only to make ourselves grander; but You create in order to have things and persons to love. And if You created us in order to bestow Your blessings on us, why wouldn't You also be so happy to bestow even greater blessings on us in Heaven? Yes, You will! Amen.

Day 20

Whom have I in heaven but Thee? And there is nothing upon earth that I desire besides thee.   —Ps. 73:25

Let us not strive for the rewards of heaven, valuable though they may be, but live so as to please the God of heaven. If God were not in heaven, all its beauty, riches, and sweetness would be dull rather than delightful. By faith, we know God already dwells within us. But in heaven we will see God face to face. May we so live that one day we will be in heaven praising and playing eternally before our Lord and Savior! —St. Jane Frances de Chantal

St. Jane of Chantal, beautiful widow Saint, even we who count ourselves among the ardently faithful have difficulty seeking God more than His gifts. We say we want God above all things, but often our desires and prayers center more on our earthly needs and cares. We believe that to love You, God, and experience Your love for us will bring us ecstatic joy. St. Jane, contemplative, intercede for us now that we may give ourselves to God and be still enough to let His love for us permeate our worried little hearts. Amen.

Day 21

[We] proclaim to you the eternal life which was with the Father and was made manifest to us.   —1 Jn. 1:2

Death is nothing else but going home to God; the bond of love will be unbroken for all eternity.   —Bl. Teresa of Calcutta

Jesus, we, your funny little sinful creatures, wonder how You could truly desire to have us with you where You are, in Heaven. But as St. John tells us, the reason that You came down to earth was to reveal that eternal life is being personally with the Trinity. It encourages us to think that your Saints, who knew You so much better than we do, truly believed that "the bond of love will be unbroken for all eternity." We may think it more humble to set our sights, at best, on Purgatory. Help us instead to respond to Your desire to be with us by yearning to be with You. Amen.

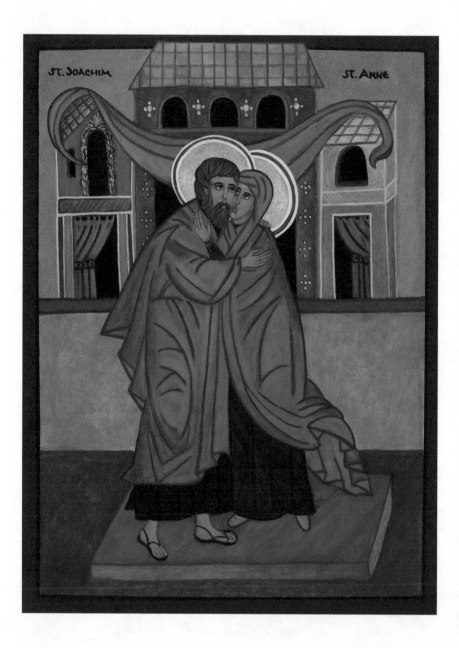

2

In Heaven, We Will Be United with Family and Friends

Few among us have not felt the vicarious sting of death when a spouse, parent, grandparent, or some other close relative or good friend has departed this life. Because we miss them, it is only natural to wonder if we will ever see them again and to fervently hope for that eventuality. In fact, among all the magnificent joys of Heaven, the one that is most frequently anticipated and eagerly longed for—second only to seeing God Himself—is the expectation of being reunited with our loved ones who have gone before us. Is this an illusory hope, or can we be sure that we will see, recognize, and love our family and friends in Heaven?

Catholics believe in the communion of Saints, defined in the glossary of the *Catechism* as "the unity in Christ of all the redeemed, those on earth and those who have died." This unity is present to all the faithful in many ways, but we experience it most acutely in the celebration of Holy Mass. In the Mass, the living are present to eternity, and eternity is present in time to the living. In the Mass, the faithful departed in the Church Triumphant, those Saints who are in Heaven (which is, of course, the definition of all those souls who are in the nearer presence of God and enjoy the Beatific Vision), as well as the souls who are in Purgatory, the members of the Church Suffering who are expectant of their eventual eternal reward, are united with the Church Militant—those Christians who are still living here on earth and are engaged in their ongoing spiritual warfare. Together these three expressions of the Church constitute the communion of Saints that we confess each week in the liturgy through recitation of the creed. In the Eucharistic celebration, the living and the dead are joined together in unity in this one mystical body. During the liturgy, the living pray for the dead in Purgatory and to the Saints in Heaven, while the souls in Heaven pray for the living. Together they enjoy a true spiritual communion. The Church says,

> To the offering of Christ are united not only the members still here on earth, but also those already in the glory of heaven. In communion with and commemorating the Blessed Virgin Mary and all the saints, the Church offers the Eucharistic sacrifice. In the Eucharist the Church is as it were at the foot of the cross with Mary, united with the offering and intercession of Christ. The Eucharistic sacrifice is also offered for the faithful departed who "have died in Christ but are not yet wholly purified," so that they may be able to enter into the light and peace of Christ.[1]

It is then, at Holy Mass, that the living faithful in this life are connected most intimately with those who have gone before them, marked with the sign of faith. Together they are united in the Eucharistic sacrifice with their deceased loved ones. They pray for each other and join together around the altar in the worship of the Lord, who is truly and substantially present in this sacred mystery.

---

1   *CCC*, 1370, 382.

This unity cements a kind of continuing spiritual bond that we enjoy with our departed loved ones even now, in this life, in a very real and vital way. Since we enjoy this sort of union with our deceased family and friends now, then in Heaven—when all is perfected, completed, and made whole—it stands to reason that the relationships we enjoyed in this life will also share in that perfection of the life to come. So long as our loved ones and we all depart this life in a state of grace and friendship with God, then the bond that we share in the communion of Saints will never be broken. Even so, will the relationship we have with our loved ones in Heaven be the same as it was here in this life? Will we recognize them?

The Sacred Scriptures indicate that there is a continuity of personal identity following death. For example, on Mount Tabor at the Transfiguration of Our Lord, Moses and Elijah were both familiar with each other (*Matt.* 17:3–4). In the story of the rich man and Lazarus, both he and Lazarus, as well as Abraham, were identifiable after death (*Luke* 16:20–24). Jesus, following His death and Resurrection, was recognized by Mary Magdalene, Thomas, and the other disciples, as well as by numerous others (*Luke* 16:20–24; *John* 20:16, 20, 24–29; 21:12; *1 Cor.* 15:4–7). So it would seem that we will hopefully be able to recognize our friends and loved ones in Heaven.

However, it does not follow that the relationships that we enjoyed in this life will be of exactly the same character in Heaven. Jesus said that in the life to come we "neither marry nor are given in marriage, but are like angels in heaven" (*Matt.* 22:30). This would appear to rule out the kind of married relationship that spouses enjoyed in this life, since the purposes of marriage are fulfilled here and are not needed in Heaven. Nevertheless, that does not mean that a husband and wife will not have a special connection in Heaven in a way that is not completely understandable now. What Jesus was rejecting was the mistaken notion that the spousal relationship in Heaven would be a straightforward continuance of the same relationship that the spouses had in this world. This would apply also, for example, to parents and their children. A mother always will be a mother and a father always will be a father, but the exact contours of those relationships may be different in Heaven than they were in this life.

Even if we cannot precisely define the quality and kind of relationships we will enjoy with our friends and loved ones in Heaven, we do know that they will be supremely and definitively happy. They will be freed from the effects of sin, death, and the devil. All the difficulties that may have marred our exchanges with each other from time to time—all our imperfections of character that we allowed to rule our behavior and interactions, all our mistakes, along with the anger and pain that we may have wreaked on each other—are destined to pass away. There, in the nearer presence of God, we will discover that "the old has passed away, behold, the new has come" (*2 Cor.* 5:17). In this wonderful state, in the presence of the God who made us, we will love each other fully and rightly, perhaps for the first time, and together "we shall always be with the Lord. Therefore comfort one another with these words" (*1 Thess.* 4:17–18).

Day 22

For God has not destined us for wrath, but to obtain salvation through our Lord Jesus Christ, who died for us so that whether we wake or sleep we might live with him.   —1 Thess. 5:9–10

Beloved brothers, let us set out for these pastures where we shall keep joyful festival with so many of our fellow citizens. May the thought of their happiness urge us on! Let us stir up our hearts, rekindle our faith, and long eagerly for what heaven has in store for us. To love thus is to be already on our way. No matter what obstacles we encounter, we must not allow them to turn us aside from the joy of that heavenly feast. Anyone who is determined to reach his destination is not deterred by the roughness of the road that leads to it. Nor must we allow the charm of success to seduce us, or we shall be like a foolish traveler who is so distracted by the pleasant meadows through which he is passing that he forgets where he is going.   —St. Gregory the Great

God the Father, so bountiful in blessings, we would be happy just to get away from the crosses of life on earth. We would be happy to have You, alone, in Heaven. You create a superabundance of good things for us on earth: not one type of flower, but thousands; not one color, but hundreds. Similarly, we are told, we will have You plus so many other wonderful things. We may never have thought of the way our own joy in being saved would be augmented by experiencing salvation *together* with those we love. As St. Gregory writes, of course it will be happiness for us to see our loved ones so happy, at last! May our guardian Angels lead us far from any sin that would impede our swift coming into such a reward. Amen.

Day 23

"Blessed are those servants whom the master finds awake when he comes; truly, I say to you, he will gird himself and have them sit at table, and he will come and serve them."—Luke 12:37

A society, sweet and delightful and lovable beyond conception! Such fellowship will intensify your joy. Arise then and speed with haste to the nuptials, because of the transcendent beauty of the servant who waits to perform your commands. That servant is not one only, for the whole angelic assembly, yea, even the very Son of God will be in readiness to attend to your wants. Listen to what He says of Himself as reported in the Holy Gospel of St. Luke: "Amen, I say to you, that He will gird Himself, and make them sit down to meat, and passing, will minister unto them." Ah, then indeed, great will be the glory of the poor and lowly, to have the Son of God, the Eternal King, ministering to their wants and the whole court of Heaven diligently obeying their behests.

—St. Bonaventure

Dear Jesus, we read of Your washing the feet of Your disciples before Your Passion or cooking fish on the shore for them after Your Resurrection. We love the paintings artists have made of these events, yet we don't really think that You will do similar humble services for us as part of our reward. May we remember this promise whenever the labor of ministering to others seems too burdensome to us. Amen.

Day 24

Welcome into the company of your saints our relatives and benefactors who have died. May we share their happiness one day.
—Evening Prayer for Friday, Week I, *Divine Office*

O Diana, what a wretched state of affairs this is, which we have to endure! Our love for each other here is never free from pain and anxiety. You are upset and hurt because you are not permitted to see me the whole time, and I am upset because your presence is so rarely granted me. I wish we could be brought into the city of the Lord of Hosts where we shall no longer be stranded from him or from each other. —Bl. Jordan of Saxony to Bl. Diana of Andalo

Dear Blesseds Jordan and Diana, saintly spiritual friends, some of us, when we dream of reunion in Heaven with those we loved on earth, think only of family. But what of those spiritual friends and mentors who helped us so greatly with compassion and advice in our struggle to become holy? Won't it be wonderful to see them smiling as we enter the gates of Heaven, so glad that their love for us bore fruit to be rewarded by the Kingdom itself? We think of each such friend now with gratitude and beg them to intercede for us that we may be reunited in the arms of Jesus. Amen.

Day 25

The king has brought me into his chambers. We will exult and rejoice in you; we will extol your love more than wine.

—*Song of Sol.* 1:4

All blessed spirits perpetually gather themselves together and form a burning flame of love, that they may fulfill this work, and that God may be loved according to his nobility.

—Bl. Jan van Ruysbroeck

Blessed Jan, Saint and mystic, in a supernatural manner you may have seen such burning flames of love made up of the spirits of all the Saints already in Heaven. Help us to value foretastes of such unified flames of love that we already experience on earth, as when an orchestra performs a glorious symphony or the flame unites in the hearts of spouses at their wedding ceremony. Father God, creator of billions of human beings, may You be glorified by us in Heaven when we sing Your praises in unison.

Day 26

Before we go our separate ways, let us take leave of our brother. May our farewell express our affection for him; may it ease our sadness and strengthen our hope. One day we shall joyfully greet him again when the love of Christ, which conquers all things, destroys even death itself. —The Mass for the Dead

Our country is heaven. There a great multitude of our friends expect us, a vast number desire our coming—secure and certain of their own salvation, and only solicitous for ours. What unspeakable comfort is it, to come to the sight and embrace of them! As himself, delights in the happiness of others, as much as in his own, and what he hath not in himself, he possesses in the society he is in: so that he hath as many joys as he has fellows in felicity; and the several joys of all are the comfort to every saint, as his own peculiar delights; and because all love God more than themselves, they take more pleasure in his bliss than of all their joys beside.
—St. Robert Southwell

Lord, we know that our primary reason for hoping for Heaven is the joy of being united with the Holy Trinity. Nevertheless, you created us as humans to love those in our families and to love our friends. We pray often for the souls of our beloved dead on their journey through Purgatory. Please, Mother Mary, remind us when we grieve for our beloved dead that one day we hope to see them again in the world without end where Your Son reigns. Amen.

Day 27

There are friends who pretend to be friends, but there is a friend who sticks closer than a brother.   —*Prov.* 18:24

Truly it is a blessed thing to love on earth as we hope to love in heaven, and to begin that friendship here which is to endure for ever there. I am not now speaking of simple charity, a love due to all mankind, but of that spiritual friendship which binds souls together, leading them to share devotions and spiritual interests, so as to have but one mind between them.   —St. Francis de Sales

Sts. Francis de Sales and Jane of Chantal, great spiritual friends and mentors to so many followers, how often you advised us to be so careful to seek out the company of holy people for inspiration. Woe to us if, even as we lavish charity on the needy, we choose as chums for relaxation only those whose minds and hearts are far from God! Intercede for us, patron Saints and Angels, that we may choose the friends we will be with forever in the land where human love is sealed eternally in a permanent state of grace. Amen.

Day 28

"Therefore are they before the throne of God, and serve him day and night within his temple; and he who sits upon the throne will shelter them with his presence."   —Rev. 7:15

I was in the greatest affliction at the loss of my son, and was consumed by a desire to know what was his position in the other world. God deigned to comfort me. About a month after his death, during a very restless night, I saw, as it were, the ceiling opened, and Dominic appeared in the midst of dazzling light. I was beside myself at this sight, and cried out: "O Dominic, pray for your brothers and sisters, and your mother and father, that we may all come to join you one day in Heaven."

"Yes, yes, I will pray," was the answer. Then he disappeared, and the room became as before.

—From the vision of Charles Savio,
father of St. Dominic,
after the death of this son.

Jesus, we are warned in Scripture and in the *Catechism* never to seek through mediums assurance of the salvation of those who have died. Yet surely you know the yearning in the heart of a family member to know that one who has died is safe! Take away any need for a specific sign of our own concoction. Give us instead the right spirit of desire to be consoled by conviction that our beloved dead live in Your presence. We thank you for any signs You have given us but wait peacefully in hope for the full consummation in Heaven of our desire for reunion. Amen.

Day 29

"I am Raphael, one of the seven holy angels who present the prayers of the saints and enter into the presence of the glory of the Holy One."   —*Tob.* 12:15

I am now ready to leave. I have my passport for heaven, and it is my dear father who has obtained this grace for me. On the twenty-ninth, he gave me the assurance that I would soon go to join him. The next day the doctor astonished by the progress the sickness had made in two days, said to Mother that this was time to grant my wish to receive Extreme Unction. So I had this happiness on the thirtieth, and also that of seeing Jesus in the Blessed Sacrament leave the tabernacle to come to me, Whom I received as Viaticum for my long voyage! This Bread of Heaven has strengthened me. Just look, it seems as if my pilgrimage can't get to its destination. Far from complaining about this, I rejoice that God still lets me suffer for love of Him. Ah, how good it is to let yourself go in His arms, which neither fears nor desires.   —Thérèse of Lisieux

Oh, Little Thérèse, you teach us that holy parents in Heaven are especially eager to help in the last days of their children on earth. We think of your anguish at the death of your mother when you were so small and then, after entering the convent, your anguish to know that your beloved father was so afflicted with illness. Would you intercede for us, St. Thérèse, that we may be healed of any remaining wounds in our relationship with our dead parents and that one day we may be reunited in Heaven?

Day 30

"[H]e will wipe away every tear from their eyes, and death shall be no more, neither shall there be mourning nor crying nor pain any more, for the former things have passed away."

—*Rev.* 21:4

What kind of heaven would it be if we didn't have with us those whom we love? The joy of paradise will be enough to carry us all on. Every sacrifice we make on earth will be recompensed. Heaven is total joy, continuous joy. We will be constantly thanking God. It's useless to try to figure out exactly what heaven is like, because we can't understand it, but when the veil of this life is taken off, we will understand things in a different way. No suffering, no matter how low the motive on which it rests, will go unrewarded in eternal life. Trust and hope in the merits of Jesus and in this way even poor clay will become finest gold which will shine in the palace of the king of heaven.   —St. Padre Pio

St. Padre Pio, who could be so stern a confessor, you seemed to have only hope for the completeness of joy in Heaven for your disciples. We marvel when you proclaim that even suffering that comes from the lowest of motives will be rewarded! Do you mean, perhaps, times when we make a small sacrifice or accept a small frustration just because we see no way out? You, St. Padre Pio, who lovingly embraced so much physical pain, pray for us weak ones that taking heart from your vision we will endure without undue complaint until the end. Amen.

Day 31

And another angel came and stood at the altar with a golden censer; and he was given much incense to mingle with the prayers of all the saints upon the golden altar before the throne.

—*Rev.* 8:3

The souls in heaven are praying for us (whom they loved) and assisting us with love made more alive in the light of glory.

—Bl. Pope John XXIII

Blessed John XXIII, such a loving fatherly man you were, in your own family and with the whole "People of God." You knew how to look past the faults of others to see their immortal souls struggling to be free of their worst enemy—themselves! Intercede for us with the love you now have in the place of "the light of glory" that we may also learn how to forgive even those who have caused us the most hurt. Amen.

3

In Heaven, We Will Be
with Angels and the Saints

One of the first prayers that many Catholic children are taught is a traditional prayer to their Guardian Angels:

Angel of God, my guardian dear,
To whom His love commits me here,
Ever this day, be at my side
To light and guard, to rule and guide.

Amen.

This beautiful little prayer (to which, by the way, a partial indulgence is attached) teaches us to be on intimate spiritual terms with our Guardian Angels. According to the *Catechism*, "From its beginning until death, human life is surrounded by [the angels'] watchful care and intercession. 'Beside each believer stands an angel as protector and shepherd leading him to life.' Already here on earth the Christian life shares by faith in the blessed company of angels and men united in God."[1] Because of the familiarity that these particular Angels have with us throughout the course of our lives, it would be my expectation

---

1   *CCC*, 336, 98.

that upon our arrival in Heaven our Guardian Angels would be one of the first to greet us. In fact, I think we have every reason to hope that our Guardian Angels even will be with us at the time of our death and usher our soul into the presence of the Almighty. But far from being an encounter that is unique, our entrance into that heavenly country will provide an opportunity for us to meet many more Angels, "myriads of myriads and thousands of thousands" (*Rev.* 5:11).

Who are these celestial beings that will be our near companions in Heaven throughout eternity? The Church teaches that "Angels are spiritual creatures who glorify God without ceasing and who serve his saving plans for other creatures: 'The angels work together for the benefit of us all.'"[2]

Throughout the Sacred Scriptures, there are numerous references regarding the ministry of Angels. The word "Angel" means "messenger," and it indicates their primary function and office in the service of God is as His servants and emissaries.

Angels are immortal and noncorporeal; they are pure spirits and thus invisible to the human eye. Therefore, when they appear to human beings with a message or mission from God, they typically take on a human form so that they can be recognized. We see this in many of the biblical accounts: the Angel sent to guard the entrance to the Garden of Eden after the fall of Adam and Eve; the three Angels who appeared to Abraham before the destruction of Sodom; the Angel who wrestled with Jacob, as well as the many Angels Jacob saw ascending and descending on a ladder that stretched into Heaven; the Angel who appeared to the priest Zechariah (the father of St. John the Baptist) as he ministered in the Temple; the Angel who announced to the Blessed Virgin Mary that she was to be the

---

2 *CCC*, 350, 101.

mother of the Messiah; the Angels who made known to the shepherds that the Saviour had been born; the Angel who assisted Jesus in His agony in the garden; the Angels who proclaimed the Resurrection of our Lord outside the empty tomb; the Angels who appeared to the disciples after the Ascension of Christ into Heaven; as well as many other examples.

Only three of the Angels are given names in the Bible: Michael, "the great prince who has charge of your people" (*Dan.* 12:1); Raphael, "one of the seven holy angels who present the prayers of the saints and enter into the presence of the glory of the Holy One" (*Tob.* 12:15); and Gabriel, who makes several appearances in Scripture, most prominently at the Annunciation: "in the sixth month the angel Gabriel was sent from God to a city of Galilee named Nazareth, to a virgin betrothed to a man whose name was Joseph, of the house of David; and the virgin's name was Mary" (*Luke* 1:26–27). It seems likely that all the Angels have names and in Heaven we may be privileged to speak to them, learn their names, and hear directly from them about the mighty acts they have undertaken on behalf of God.

Based on the writings of certain early Church theologians (with whom St. Thomas Aquinas later was in agreement), nine choirs of Angels have been identified from the highest to the lowest in the angelic hierarchy: seraphim, cherubim, thrones, dominations, virtues, powers, principalities, archangels, and angels. Michael, Raphael, and Gabriel have been traditionally identified as archangels, along with Uriel, who makes an appearance in the noncanonical Book of Enoch. Wouldn't it be wonderful to hear the amazing stories that these Angels could tell, not only of their works within human history, but outside of time as well? I can just imagine myself seeking an audience in Heaven with the Archangel Gabriel to inquire about the wonderful details of his involvement in the Annunciation!

But there could be an even more amazing conversation than that. What if we could sit down and have a long discussion with the Blessed Virgin Mary herself, the Queen of Angels and Saints? Not only would we have the perspective of Gabriel regarding that event, but we would have her primary source information as well! And it is an experience such as this that the glory of Heaven promises to all the redeemed. For not only will we have as our company all the myriads of Angels, but we will also enjoy as our companions all the Saints of every era and place.

Of course, we Christians who remain at this time on earth in the Church Militant already share in a sure and certain fellowship with Christians in the Church Suffering (Purgatory), as well as those Christians in the Church Triumphant (Heaven). As we profess each week in the Creed when we say we believe in the communion of Saints, we mean that we believe "in the communion of all the faithful of Christ, those who are pilgrims on earth, the dead who are being purified, and the blessed in heaven, all together forming one Church; and we believe that in this communion, the merciful love of God and his saints is always [attentive] to our prayers."[3]

But at the last, when the end of the ages has come and all the redeemed stand in the nearer presence of God, this fellowship will be perfected and entirely realized. We will then be able to know fully and completely our Mother, the Blessed Virgin Mary, and all those holy ones whose names we so often commemorate in the Roman Canon of the sacred liturgy: "John the Baptist, Stephen, Matthias, Barnabas, Ignatius, Alexander, Marcellinus, Peter, Felicity, Perpetua, Agatha, Lucy, Agnes, Cecilia,

---

3   *CCC*, 962.

Anastasia, and all the saints."[4] This is because "the multitude of those gathered around Jesus and Mary in Paradise forms the Church of heaven, where in eternal blessedness they see God as he is and where they are also, to various degrees, associated with the holy angels in the divine governance exercised by Christ in glory, by interceding for us and helping our weakness by their fraternal concern."[5]

To know directly, love fully, and be fully loved by all the Angels and Saints of every time and every place for all eternity, all in the surpassing presence and intimacy of the Beatific Vision of God—what better definition of Heaven could there be?

---

4   Roman Missal, The Sacramentary, New York: Catholic Book Publishing, 1985, Eucharistic Prayer 1, (the Roman Canon), 547.
5   *CCC*, 1053, 297.

Day 32

It is the Spirit himself bearing witness with our spirit that we are children of God, and if children, then heirs, heirs of God and fellow heirs with Christ, provided we suffer with him in order that we may also be glorified with him.   —*Rom.* 8:16–17

We had suffered, he said, and we passed out of the flesh, and we began to be carried towards the east by four angels. And passing over the world's edge we saw a very great light; and I said to Perpetua (for she was at my side): "This which the Lord promised us; we have received His promise." And while we were being carried by these same four angels, a great space opened before us. And there in the garden were four other angels, more glorious than the rest; who when they saw us gave us honor and said to the other angels: "Lo, here are they, here are they": and marveled. The other angels said to us: 'Come first, go in, and salute the Lord,' and we went in, and we heard as it were one voice crying Sanctus, Sanctus, Sanctus, without any end. And I said to Perpetua: "You have that which you desire." And she said to me: "Yes, God be thanked; so that I that was glad in the flesh am now more glad."

—From a vision of Heaven given to
Saturus after the martyrdom of St. Perpetua

Truly, Lord, we are amazed to think that a vision from the earliest days of the martyr Church would be preserved unto our century to give us hope as we move toward the end of our lives on earth! Even in our times, there are some who claim to have seen Angels. This makes it easier for them to seek the Angels' guidance. We who must go by faith thank You for the precious legacy of visions of the holy ones. We beg You, give us a glimpse of the Angels now if that will help us one day after death to get to their abode. Amen.

Day 33

For he will give his angels charge over you to guard you in all
your ways   —*Ps.* 91:11

These words should fill you with respect, inspire devotion
and instill confidence; respect for the presence of the angels, devo-
tion because of their loving service, and confidence because of their
protection. We should then show our affection for the angels, for
one day they will be our co-heirs just as here below they are our
guardians and trustees appointed and set over us by the Father.
We are God's children although it does not seem so, because we are
still but small children under guardians and trustees, and for the
present little better than slaves.   —St. Bernard

St. Bernard, how different was your vision from that of
some mystics who thought of life after death as "the alone to the
Alone."[6] From the study of Scripture and tradition, and from
their own personal prayers, the Doctors of the Church knew
that Heaven would be a glorious communion of many levels
of being. Jesus tells us of Angels chosen to guard each of us on
earth. Should we not rejoice in the thought that someday we
will be in the company of such Angels, together praising the
Holy Trinity? Let us start right now by praying to our Angels
for a greater sense of the heavenly realities that await us. Amen.

Day 34

All-powerful Father, as now we bring you our songs of praise, so may we sing your goodness in the company of your saints forever. We ask this through our Lord Jesus Christ, your Son, who lives and reigns with you and the Holy Spirit, one God, forever and ever.
                                                    —From *Liturgy of the Hours*, Week II

We long to share in the citizenship of heaven, to dwell with the spirits of the blessed. In short we long to be united in happiness with all the saints.   —St. Bernard

Dear Holy Spirit, sanctifier, we ask the Saints to intercede for us every day. We have baptismal Saints, confirmation Saints, patron Saints for special needs, and other favorites. We can feel tremulous and even shy at the idea of actually seeing them someday face-to-face. This is because we know we love them, but it is hard for us to imagine that they love us. Yet Mother Church teaches us that they do, indeed, love us and long more than anything to help by their prayers to bring us into their glorious company. Help us now to picture each one of the Saints we know about and rejoice in the thought of being with them forever in Heaven. Amen.

Day 35

So then you are no longer strangers and sojourners, but you are fellow citizens with the saints and members of the household of God.
                                                            —*Eph.* 2:19

Come for all the saints are waiting for you with great joy.
                    —Jesus to Bl. Angela, in the last week of her life

Dear Saints, will you really be waiting for us at the gates of Heaven? In our humorous way, we picture St. Peter's vestibule because Jesus gave him the keys to the Kingdom of Heaven. And we like to picture our loved ones, especially any so holy that we think (mistakenly or not) have long gotten through Purgatory. Rarely, though, do we picture the Saints waiting for us at the gates of eternity at the very moment of our death. Even though we know that private locutions to the Saints, such as these, are not universal teachings of the Faith, we ask the Holy Spirit to give us a foretaste of these eternal joys to come. Amen.

Day 36

We are all members of one another.   —*Eph.* 4:25

Just as in a physical body the operation of one member con-
tributes to the good of the whole body, so it is in a spiritual body
such as the Church the good of one member is communicated to
another, as the Apostle says. For that reason, among the points of
faith handed down by the Apostles, is that there is a community
of goods in the Church, and this is expressed in the words Com-
munion of Saints. This is in accordance with divine order, which
makes higher things react upon lower things, like the brightness of
the sun filling the atmosphere.   —St. Thomas Aquinas

Apostles of the Church, we ask you to intercede for us
poor earthlings! How is it that we say the words of the Creed,
"we believe in the communion of saints," yet so few of us talk
about one day being among you in Heaven? May the Lord bap-
tize our imaginations so that what is on our lips may be also in
our hearts and in our minds. Amen.

Day 37

"Just so, I tell you, there will be more joy in heaven over one sinner who repents than over ninety-nine righteous persons who need no repentance."   —*Luke* 15:7

[Souls in Heaven] have not lost their love, but have it still, participating closely, with more abundance, the one with the other. For, when the soul arrives at eternal life, all participate in the good of that soul, and the soul in their good . . . they have an exultation, a mirthfulness, a jubilee, a joyousness in themselves, which is refreshed by the knowledge that they have found in that soul. They see that, by My mercy, she is raised from the earth with the plenitude of grace, and therefore they exult in Me in the good of that soul, which good she has received through My goodness.
                      —From the *Dialogue of St. Catherine of Siena*

St. Catherine of Siena, Doctor of the Church, send us graces to increase our faith in these mysteries. In our experiences now, we know how much joy we take in the joy of beloved persons. Rarely are we so busy hugging a joy to ourselves that we do not want to augment that joy by sharing it; "Let's go celebrate!" we shout out when our joy overflows. Why should the Angels and Saints in Heaven not invite themselves to the great celebration of our joy in being saved? Yes, Amen.

Day 38

*"These are they who have come out of the great tribulation;
they have washed their robes and made them white in the blood of
the Lamb. Therefore are they before the throne of God."*

—*Rev.* 7:14–15

*How great is the contentment of their abode, without fear
of dying, and with eternity of living! There is the glorious choir
of apostles. The company of rejoicing prophets, the innumerable
multitude of martyrs, crowned for the victory over their passions,
and for their bloody frays. There are the troops of fair virgins.*

—St. Robert Southwell

Dear beloved, admired Saints, how we love to read about
your triumphs over sin and fear! It seems impossible that "lowly
we," who feel so inferior to you, will one day be seeing you and
conversing with you. And since we so often begged your intercession, even you will be rejoicing over our graceful triumphs
over sin and fear. Yes, yes, yes! Today please ask that we may have
a little extra boost of faith, hope, and charity. Amen.

Day 39

I have fought the good fight.   *—2 Tim.* 4:7

How great will the glory be for that just soul to be placed with such an infinite multitude of angels, on the very throne of Christ and of God! And how will this soul exult with gladness, when, delivered from every toil and danger, she shall behold herself gloriously triumphant over all her enemies! Were we to behold, in this our exile, one angel arrayed in all his beauty, who would not eagerly wish to meet him? What therefore must it be, to behold all the angels in one place? And if only one of the prophets, apostles, or doctors of the Church were to descend from heaven, with what curiosity and attention would he be heard! Now in the kingdom of God, we shall be allowed to behold not one only, but all the prophets, apostles, and doctors, with whom we shall continually hold sweet converse. How greatly does the sun rejoice the whole earth: but what will be the glory from innumerable Suns in the kingdom of God, all animate, intelligent, and exulting in their joy! This union with the angels and men, all of whom are most wise and excellent, appears to me so delightful, that I consider it alone will be a great happiness, and on this account, would willingly be deprived of all the pleasures of this life. —St. Robert Bellarmine

St. Robert, most of us modern Catholics avoid thinking about Heaven as triumph over enemies! Yes, perhaps when we think of Christian martyrs or soldiers in faraway lands, but not in our usual circumstances. Far from most of us are images of the daily spiritual warfare we need to be engaged in to avoid sin.

But you, St. Robert, Doctor of the Church, teach us that part of our Heaven will be the joy of being with the victorious Angels and Saints. Help us to fight the good fight, so as to win. Amen.

Day 40

So God created man in his own image, in the image of God he created him; male and female he created them. —Gen. 1:27

There is a spiritual life that we share with the angels of heaven, for like them we have been formed in the image and likeness of God. —St. Lawrence of Brindisi

Father, Creator of Heaven and earth, how we love the poetic beauty of those phrases in the book of Genesis about Adam and Eve being created in the image and likeness of You! Yet they leave most of us bewildered. We know that "image and likeness" doesn't mean that You, pure spirit, have a body. Most Christian philosophers interpret "image and likeness" to mean that we are created like the Angels, with a spiritual component of mind, heart, and will, or that like the Trinity, we are persons destined for self-giving love. May we long for Your eternity where our fellowship with the Angels will be so clear in the nature of our being and in our love. Amen.

Day 41

And a great portent appeared in heaven, a woman clothed with the sun, with the moon under her feet, and on her head a crown of twelve stars. —*Rev.* 12:1

To you it yet remains to labor on earth for the glory of your Redeemer, and to make up your eternal crown. I do not leave you to abandon you, but to help you still more in heaven by my intercession with God. Be satisfied. I commend the holy Church to you; I commend redeemed souls to you; let this be my last farewell, and the only remembrance I leave you: execute it if you love me, labor for the good of souls and for the glory of my Son; for one day we shall meet again in Paradise, never more for all eternity to be separated.

—Words attributed to Mary at her Assumption, by Saint Alphonsus de Liguori

Dear Mary, our Mother, Queen of Angels and Saints, great will be our joy in Heaven to finally see you face-to-face, you our greatest intercessor. Some critics of Catholic doctrine think of our Church as too masculine. All the Saints have imitated you in love; we pray that each of us may ever grow in trust in your love for us and that we may help those spiritually orphaned on the maternal side to seek and accept you, as well. Amen.

Day 42

Hail, holy Queen, Mother of mercy, our life, our sweetness and our hope. To thee do we cry, poor banished children of Eve, to thee do we send up our sighs, mourning and weeping in this valley of tears. Turn then, most gracious Advocate, thine eyes of mercy toward us, and after this our exile, show unto us the blessed fruit of thy womb, Jesus. O clement, O loving, O sweet Virgin Mary!

—"The Salve Regina"

O most sweet Lady and our Mother, thou hast already left the earth and reached thy kingdom, where, as Queen, thou art enthroned above all the choirs of angels, as the Church sings: "She is exalted above the choirs of angels in the celestial kingdom." Remember that in leaving this world thou didst promise not to forget us. See in the midst of what tempests and dangers we constantly are, and shall be until the end of our lives. By the merits of thy happy death obtain us holy perseverance in the divine friendship, that we may finally quit this life in God's grace; and thus we also shall one day come to kiss thy feet in Paradise, and unite with the blessed spirits in praising thee and singing thy glories as thou deserves.

—Saint Alphonsus de Liguori

Oh, Saint Alphonsus, when we read about the last decades of your life on earth, full of pain and problems, we realize that these words are not mere pious expressions. No, your pleas that your mother in Heaven would help you in holy perseverance came from a heart filled with anguish, as are many of ours when we enter into the last years of our lives. How consoling is your image of kissing Mary's feet in Heaven while the Angels sing!

May you be there also to greet us as we fall at the feet of Mary in thanksgiving. Amen.

Day 43

Hail Mary, full of grace. Our Lord is with thee. Blessed art thou among women, and blessed is the fruit of thy womb, Jesus. Holy Mary, Mother of God, pray for us sinners, now and at the hour our death. Amen. —"The Salve Regina"

Love Mary! She is loveable, faithful, constant. She will never let herself be outdone in love, but will ever remain supreme. If you are in danger, she will hasten to free you. If you are troubled, she will console you. If you are sick, she will bring you relief. If you are in need, she will help you. She does not look to see what kind of person you have been. She simply comes to a heart that wants you to love her. She comes quickly and opens her merciful heart to you, embraces you and consoles and serves you. She will even be at hand to accompany you on the trip to eternity.

—St. Gabriel of Our Lady of Sorrows

Mother Mary in Heaven, you must think of us, your children, as very stupid. Many of those who will read this book say fifty Hail Marys a day, ending with "pray for us sinners, now and at the hour of our death." Yet when we picture the hour of our deaths, we allow ourselves, at least sometimes, to think of grisly physical details and not of you accompanying us, as your Saint tells us you will! Please be with us not only at the hour of our deaths but at every moment of our lives, especially when we are anxious and afraid. Amen.

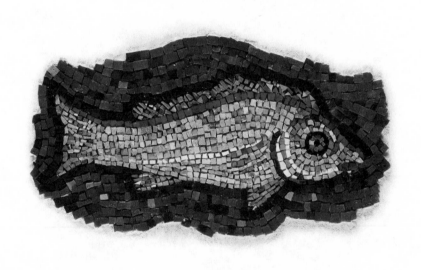

4

In Heaven, We Will Live in Beauty That Surpasses Nature

What does Heaven look like? What is its topography? Are there oceans? What about rivers, lakes, trees, plants, animals, and mountains? Will we see all those as well? Are the streets really paved with gold and are the gates of the city made of pearl? Where is Heaven located? All these questions, to one extent or another, reflect images taken from the Sacred Scriptures themselves, images that seek to describe the indescribable in terms that human beings can understand. By making use of symbolic and poetic language—as well as using illustrative, allegorical, and figurative terms—the inspired writers sought to capture the essential, inexpressible beauty and joy of Heaven, the true reality of which is only palely reflected in the glories of the created order.

In fact, Heaven is not a place at all. It does not have a location or address as we might commonly understand it. Instead, Heaven is a spiritual state of being that exists beyond the temporal order that our human senses can perceive. It does, without doubt, truly exist, but it encompasses a spiritual existence and not a merely physical one. As St. Thomas Aquinas put it, "Incorporeal things are not in place after a manner known and familiar to us, in which way we say that bodies are properly in place; but they are in place after a manner befitting spiritual substances, a manner that cannot be fully manifest to us."[1]

This understanding is echoed by Pope John Paul II, who stated in his general audience of July 21, 1999, that "Heaven is neither an abstraction nor a physical place in the clouds, but a living, personal relationship with the Holy Trinity. It is our meeting with the Father which takes place in the risen Christ through the communion of the Holy Spirit."

So the essential characteristic of Heaven is the relationship that the souls of the redeemed enjoy with God. It is a spiritual relationship that all Christ's faithful, who die in the state of grace, will eventually experience in a condition of perfect happiness and fulfillment. Heaven is that experience where the righteous behold God face-to-face in the Beatific Vision forever and ever. This is the greatest joy and good of Heaven. According to the *Catechism*, "This perfect life with the Most Holy Trinity— this communion of life and love with the Trinity, with the Virgin Mary, the angels and all the blessed—is called 'heaven.' Heaven is the ultimate end and fulfillment of the deepest human longings, the state of supreme, definitive happiness."[2]

Because Heaven is a spiritual existence, it would seem to follow that physical things, all those material objects and creatures of the world that belong to the natural created order, cannot be a part of the purely spiritual life that is Heaven. Or can they? In fact, the Church has infallibly pronounced about two individuals who do retain a glorified physical as well as spiritual existence in Heaven: our Lord Jesus Christ, who ascended into Heaven, and his mother, the Blessed Virgin Mary, who was assumed into Heaven, with both body and soul. Additionally,

---

1   *Summa Theologiae*, Supplement, Q69, a1, reply 1.
2   *CCC*, 1024, 289.

the Old Testament points to the possibility that the prophets Elijah and Enoch may have been taken—body and soul—into Heaven, and some traditions include Moses in that number as well, but these are only pious speculations. How these retain both body and soul in a spiritual state of existence is not fully understandable but is a surety left to the mystery of faith.

Clearly, however, the eternal destiny of the redeemed faithful is not a disembodied existence. Rather, at the end of time, after the General Resurrection from the dead, there will be a new Heaven and a new earth, where the souls of the faithful departed, rejoined with their redeemed physical bodies (along with the righteous people who are alive and remain at this time), will enjoy forever a renewed, sanctified, and transfigured existence—one that is both a glorified physical and spiritual state. This wonderful transformation not only will encompass the bodies and souls of the just but will also include the natural world itself. As St. Paul put it,

> For the creation waits with eager longing for the revealing of the sons of God; for the creation was subjected to futility, not of its own will but by the will of him who subjected it in hope; because the creation itself will be set free from its bondage to decay and obtain the glorious liberty of the children of God. We know that the whole creation has been groaning in travail together until now; and not only the creation, but we ourselves, who have the first fruits of the Spirit, groan inwardly as we wait for adoption as sons, the redemption of our bodies. (*Rom.* 8:19–23)

More will be said about this in the next chapter, which concerns the General Resurrection.

But questions still persist, and one of the most frequently asked questions about Heaven, one that is often inquired about with the most passion, is whether or not animals—in particular, beloved pets—will be in Heaven. This issue touches sensitive nerves and is difficult to answer. Taking into account the strong emotional attachment that many people have to their pets, and given that the Magisterium of the Church has not provided a direct teaching about this subject, whatever answer one might attempt to give to this question will most probably not be met with universal acclaim.

Nevertheless, the Church does affirm certain principles that assist us in thinking critically about this question as we seek to reach a sound answer. First among those principles is the teaching that all living things have a soul. Human beings, plants, insects, animals, angels, and so forth—all of them have souls. This is to say simply that all these living beings are animated with a life force that comes from God. They are all alive and in this fashion they share a commonality. However, the Church makes a distinction between angelic and human souls and those of the lower living creatures, such as plants and animals. The Fourth Lateran Council taught that angelic souls were purely and only spiritual; the souls of animals, plants and other lower creatures were purely and only corporeal, or material; while human beings are both spiritual and material—a spiritual soul and a material body— united in one human nature: "The profession of faith of the Fourth Lateran Council (1215) affirms that God 'from the beginning of time made at once (*simul*) out of nothing both orders of creatures, the spiritual and the corporeal, that is, the angelic and the earthly, and then (*deinde*) the human creature, who as it were shares in both orders, being composed of spirit and body.'"[3] The

---

3   *CCC*, 327, 95.

merely material souls of plants, animals, and other lower creatures cease to exist when they die. The spiritual souls of angels and human beings, however, are immortal. Although the bodies of human beings will eventually die and return to the dust from which they were created, their souls will live eternally. Even so, the human body that dies and decays itself will eventually be united again with its immortal soul in the Resurrection on the last day.

This, however, cannot be said of animals that die. Their material souls simply cease to exist. Does this mean that we will never see our beloved pets again? Perhaps not.

Though not a Catholic, the noted English writer C. S. Lewis hazarded a guess about the possibility of seeing our pets after the Resurrection as part of the redeemed and renewed natural order, and I think that he just might be onto something. In his collection *Letters to an American Lady*, Lewis wrote,

> I venture the supposal—it can be nothing more—that as we are raised in Christ, so at least some animals are raised in us. Who knows, indeed, but that a great deal even of the inanimate creation is raised in the redeemed souls who have, during this life, taken in its beauty into themselves? That may be the way in which the new heaven and the new earth are formed. Of course we can only guess and wonder. But these particular guesses arise in me, I trust, from taking seriously the resurrection of the body.

A new Heaven and earth implies the presence of natural beauty: skies and oceans, plants and animals. Thus, in the resurrected life, if we desire to see our beloved pets once again, those creatures that we loved and that were so important to us in our mortal lives, then we could certainly ask God if this might be so. And God, in His infinite mercy and compassion, might certainly grant such a request. It would be like God to do just such a thing. And why is that? Because God is perfect love. I am persuaded that if we have ever loved anything in a way that is commendable and pleasing to God, such a worthy love will not disappear. God does not waste anything that is good and noble, least of all love. Although one cannot say that this is a sure and certain hope, it is nonetheless a hope for which one may piously and devoutly pray.

Day 44

We know that the whole creation has been groaning in travail together until now; and not only the creation, but we ourselves who have the first fruits of the Spirit groan inwardly as we wait for adoption as sons, the redemption of our bodies. —Rom. 8:22–23

We pray thee, O Lord, for the humble beasts and for the wild animals, whom thou hast made, strong and beautiful; we supplicate for them thy great tenderness of heart, for thou hast promised to save both man and beast. —St. Basil

We thank you, St. Basil, for this sweet prayer. Some of us who have pets, or love wild animals, fear that we will never see such as these when we leave this earth. This is because the scriptures that allude to the participation of animals in Heaven are not very clear about their individual destiny. Certainly our hope of seeing them in a glorified state is not based on some false notion that they are persons with souls as we are. Nonetheless, we are taught that it is not wrong to hope they will also be saved. Please intercede for us that we may neither love animals inordinately nor detach ourselves from them as if they were too inferior to us to even count in the Kingdom of God. Instead of these false alternatives, we thank our Creator God for these precious beasts and ask the Holy Spirit for further enlightenment about their participation in eternal life. Amen.

Day 45

The wolf shall dwell with the lamb, and the leopard shall lie down with the kid, and the calf and the lion and the fatling together, and a little child shall lead them.   —Is. 11:6

Every creature which was created by you will be renewed at the Resurrection, that day which is the last day of earthly existence and the beginning of our heavenly life.
    —Attributed to St. Gregory of Narek

Holy Spirit, we wonder: what does it mean for every creature to be "renewed"? We imagine that it will be like the Garden of Eden, where we believe the animals did not depend on violence for food. What more will that renewal entail? We seem to hear You, Holy Spirit, say in our hearts that there is nothing wrong with speculating about this matter, so long as it does not become a distraction from the more important mission of evangelizing human beings. Amen.

Day 46

See how a new creation is brought at last to birth,
A new and glorious heaven, a new and glorious earth.

—*Liturgy of the Hours,*
"Hymn for Common of Holy
Women, Morning Prayer"

Man is not a being isolated from the rest of creation; by his
very nature he is bound up with the whole of the universe. In his
way to union with God, man in no way leaves creatures aside, but
gathers together in his love the whole cosmos disordered by sin, that
it may be transfigured by grace.   —St. Maximus the Confessor

St. Maximus, you taught in the Church during the time
when theologians were greatly influenced by Greek and Roman
philosophers. Some of these believed that all beings, including
animals and plants, descended from an absolute source and then
ascend upward through the contemplative appreciation of holy
sages. Such speculations, baptized into Christian understanding, suggest that our graced love for animals and plants can help
them as they are transfigured into a new creation in Heaven.
In such a spirit, inspire us to praise the Lord every time we are
delighted by lower creatures. In this way, our weary hearts can
be refreshed and also uplifted. Amen.

Day 47

And I heard every creature in heaven and on earth and under the earth and in the sea, and all therein, saying, "To Him who sits upon the throne and to the Lamb be blessing and honor and glory and might for ever and ever!"   —*Rev.* 5:13

In everything, whether it is a thing sensed or a thing known, God Himself is hidden within.   —St. Bonaventure

Holy Spirit, we read these words of the Book of Revelation and wonder if they are to be taken literally. If St. Bonaventure is correct that God Himself is hidden within everything we see or know, it certainly seems possible that in some way even the dumb beasts will shout Your praises. When we hear the sounds of nature—birds singing, ocean waves pounding, animals making their own characteristic sounds—let us be the ones to contribute those awesome words: "To the one who sits on the throne and to the Lamb be blessing and honor, glory and might, forever and ever," Amen.

Day 48

For in him all the fullness of God was pleased to dwell, and through him to reconcile to himself all things, whether on earth or in heaven, making peace by the blood of his cross. —Col. 1:20–21

That their vision may be refreshed by the beauty of the variety of creature, by redeeming mankind He restored not only man but all creatures without exception—inasmuch as all creatures are bettered through man's restoration. We believe all corporeal things to have been made for man's sake, in two ways: first, as sustenance to his bodily life, secondly, as helping him to know God, inasmuch as man sees the invisible things of God by the things that are made. Hence those bodies also will need to receive a greater inflow from the Divine goodness than now, so as to add a certain perfection of glory: and such will be the renewal of the world.

—St. Thomas Aquinas

St. Thomas, we read your words and we think about specific parts of nature we wish to see bettered: no more earthquakes, no animals killing and eating other animals, and no more biting insects. You tell us that the natural beings were created not only to serve us but also to allow us to see your beauty in theirs. How happy will we be in Heaven to look at them in a glorified state without the slightest blemish or ferocity. Thank you for sharing this wisdom with us. Amen.

Day 49

"Behold I create new heavens and a new earth, and the former things shall not be remembered."   —Is. 65:17

Then I saw a new heaven and a new earth; for the first heaven and the first earth had passed away.   —Rev. 21:1

"Every beast loveth its like" (Sirach 13:19), wherefore it is evident that likeness is the reason of love. Now man has some likeness to the universe, wherefore he is called "a little world." Hence man loves the whole world naturally and consequently desires its good. Therefore, that man's desire be satisfied the universe must needs also be made better.   —St. Thomas Aquinas

Father God, what are we to make of this insight of St. Thomas? We ponder the words and we have to agree that, indeed, there is nothing in the rest of creation that is not in some way also like us, for we have similar parts to animals, and parts of us that grow like plants, and some watery, rock- and metal-like parts. But we don't like the parts that are defective after the Fall. We don't want in Heaven to deal with decay, or floods, or sharpness. Of course, we want, instead, to see all these creatures in full perfect glory. May it be so. Amen.

Day 50

The light of the moon shall be as the light of the sun, and the light of the sun shall be sevenfold.   —Is. 30:36

The whole world will be renewed for the better. But the heaven is the more noble part of the corporeal world. Therefore it will be altered for the better. But this cannot be unless it shine out with greater brightness. Therefore its brightness will be bettered and will increase. After the resurrection, however, when the light of the moon will be increased in very truth, there will be night nowhere on earth but only in the center of the earth, where hell will be.   —St. Thomas Aquinas

St. Thomas, we are astounded. Give grace to our imaginations to move from times we can remember when the moon and sun were pale, not brilliant. And then days when the sun was especially beautiful or nights when the moon was especially brilliant. We cannot picture them seven times more wonderful! Help us to take seriously Scripture about the new Heaven and earth, and have faith that it will indeed be better than anything so far seen. Amen.

Day 51

The mountains and the hills before you shall break forth into singing, and all the trees of the field shall clap their hands.

—Is. 55:12

Glorious, indeed, will be the spring time of the Resurrection, when all that seemed dry and withered will bud forth and blossom. The glory of Lebanon will be given it, the excellency of Carmel and Sharon; the fir tree for the thorn, the myrtle tree for the briar; and the mountains and the hills shall break forth before us in singing. Who would miss being of that company?

—Bl. John Henry Cardinal Newman

God the Father, if Your servant Blessed Cardinal Newman, who was a musician himself, prophesied that the mountains and hills will be able to sing in Heaven, can we not believe it possible? All things are possible with You. Who can read these words without the heart leaping with joy? Yes, we will. Amen.

Day 52

And before the throne there is as it were a sea of glass, like
crystal.   —*Rev.* 4:6

A sea before
The Throne is spread;—its pure still glass
Pictures all earth-scenes as they pass.
We, on its shore,
Share, in the bosom of our rest,
God's knowledge, and are blest.

—Bl. John Henry Cardinal Newman

Thank you, Blessed Cardinal Newman, for this lovely image. For many of us, standing or sitting on the shoreline of lakes and oceans brings us closest to God this side of Heaven. You want to teach us to be a little more detached from what we see on the passing scene, often so terrible and ugly. Far be it from you, such a keen observer of history, to deny hellish realities. Still, we must not become mesmerized by the dark side. Intercede for us, dear poet Saint, to the more absolute truth—to God's vision. Amen.

Day 53

I consider that the sufferings of this present time are not worth comparing with the glory that is to be revealed to us.

—*Rom.* 8:18

When I was at Kriekrz to replace one of the sisters for a short time, I went across the garden one afternoon and stopped on the shore of the lake; I stood there for a long time, contemplating my surroundings. Suddenly I saw the Lord near me, and He graciously said to me, "All this I created for you; know that all this beauty is nothing compared to what I have prepared for you in eternity." Oh, how the infinitely good God pursues us with His goodness! It often happens that the Lord grants me the greatest graces when I do not at all expect them.   —St. Faustina

Holy Spirit of Surprises! When we are sick, disabled, old, or discouraged, life can seem monotonous. But then something unexpected happens—a beloved song heard on radio or TV; a charming flower at the altar; the comforting touch of a compassionate hand. So if Jesus really told Sister Faustina that the beauty of what is on earth is nothing to what we will see in eternity, help us see each of the surprises we experience now as foretastes of the great surprises to come. Amen.

Day 54

Creation itself will be set free from its bondage to decay and obtain the glorious liberty of the children of God.   —Rom. 8:21

If it will make us happy in heaven, then our dogs will be there with us.   —Servant of God Archbishop Fulton Sheen

Dear Archbishop Sheen, you surely understood the need so many of us feel to believe not that there will just be representatives of each species of animal in Heaven, but that the specific one we loved so dearly will be there. We don't have any proof of this, so pray for us that we might come to understanding and peace about this. We offer to you, God, our deep thanksgiving for those dear pets and humbly pray that our wish would be granted. Amen.

5

In Heaven, We Will Have Resurrected Bodies

Most of us have had the experience of standing at the graveside of someone we love as we commit their lifeless body to the earth. It is a sad experience, and the grief that we feel at such a loss can be intense. Much of that grief is centered in the profound absence of their presence—their physical presence. We know that we will no longer be able to hear that familiar voice, look upon that beloved face, or be comforted by that much-loved touch. It is precisely their absent company—the enforced deprivation of all the embodied joys, sorrows, challenges, and experiences of life that we shared with them in the flesh—that pains us so deeply at the time of death.

And as if that were not enough, when we allow ourselves to reflect upon this reality we realize that this very same rending of body and soul, this same imposed eradication of the physicality of life, will also one day happen to us. Regardless of how many times we are told that death is a natural part of life, it seems we are always left with the feeling that it shouldn't be, that human beings were not made for death and that it is in fact most unnatural to lose one's body to the ignominy of the grave.

To be sure, those of us who are Christians and who die in the state of grace can look forward to the inexpressible spiritual

joys and glories of Heaven, either immediately or after purification in Purgatory (see Appendix C for details about the Church's
teaching regarding Purgatory). The greatest joy of Heaven will
be the gift of beholding God face-to-face in the Beatific Vision.
Our dying ushers us into this happiness. Nonetheless, to enjoy
even such a glorious spiritual existence as that in the end—
perfectly happy and fulfilled, though without possessing our
physical bodies—would be an incomplete experience. That is to
say, it would not be as God has always intended it to be.

Because the soul has a God-given predilection for the
body, its permanent severance from the body would be unnatural. God created human beings with a spiritual soul and a material body united in one human nature. Embodied spirits—this
is who we were always meant to be before sin and death entered
into our reality through the disobedience and fall of our first
parents. Although the disembodied soul enjoying the Beatific
Vision in Heaven would not feel the lack of anything, it is God,
in His infinite goodness and mercy, who desires that His original intention for human beings be fulfilled. And in the end,
this is precisely what will happen in that coming future event
known as the General Resurrection from the dead.

St. Paul describes this glorious event in these words: "Lo!
I tell you a mystery. We shall not all sleep, but we shall all be
changed, in a moment, in the twinkling of an eye, at the last
trumpet. For the trumpet will sound, and the dead will be raised
imperishable, and we shall be changed. For this perishable nature
must put on the imperishable, and this mortal nature must put
on immortality. When the perishable puts on the imperishable,
and the mortal puts on immortality, then shall come to pass the
saying that is written: 'Death is swallowed up in victory'" (*1 Cor.*
15:51–54). In each of the historic professions of faith that the
Church has used—the Apostles' Creed, the Nicene Creed, and

the Athanasian Creed—the Resurrection of the body is proclaimed. The Faith of the Church about the Resurrection of the
body is this: that at the end of time, when our Lord Jesus Christ
returns to the earth to judge the living and the dead, He will
physically, bodily raise from the dead everyone who has died
and rejoin to each of those bodies the immortal soul that had
been severed from it at the time of its death. These resurrected
bodies will not be new creations, but the exact same bodies that
had previously lived upon the earth—with a difference. As St.
Paul describes it, the resurrected bodies of the redeemed will
be changed. They will be transformed and made to be imperishable and immortal. In the Resurrection, redeemed human
nature—body and soul together—will be glorified and transfigured into a perfect spiritual body.

This resurrected body will never die. It will not endure
illness, pain, or want. It will be free from suffering and sin, and
in some mysterious way that is not completely understandable
to those of us who await this wonderful event, it will even share
in the attributes of the resurrected body of the Lord Jesus. As St.
John put it, "Beloved, we are God's children now; it does not yet
appear what we shall be, but we know that when he appears we
shall be like him, for we shall see him as he is" (*1 Jn.* 3:2). And
again, as St. Paul notes, "[he] will change our lowly body to be
like his glorious body, by the power which enables him even to
subject all things to himself" (*Phil.* 3:21).

What might some of those attributes be? Like the Lord
Jesus, the resurrected bodies of the righteous will be endowed
with "glory" and "brightness." We remember the glorious
appearance of the Lord Jesus at the time of the Transfiguration
where "his face shone like the sun, and his garments became
white as light" (*Matt.* 17:1). This is our destiny as the children of
light, for as St. Paul says, our resurrected bodies will be "raised

in glory," (*1 Cor.* 15:43) and as St. Matthew puts it, "the righteous will shine like the sun in the kingdom of their Father" (*Matt.* 13:43) The standards of physical human beauty that are admired in contemporary society will seem as but pale, faint, and inadequate reflections of the beauty that will radiate from the resurrected bodies of even the lowliest of the redeemed, each of whom will shine with a different degree of glory according to what that particular person merited in this life: "There is one glory of the sun, and another glory of the moon, and another glory of the stars; for star differs from star in glory. So is it with the resurrection of the dead" (*1 Cor.* 15:41).

Moreover, in the Resurrection the bodies of the righteous are, as St. Paul states, "sown in weakness [but] shall rise in power" (*1 Cor.* 15:43). And since these bodies will be perfect spiritual bodies, this suggests that the physical limitations that human beings must endure in this present life (e.g., weakness, slowness, confinement to place and time, etc.) will be lessened or removed in the resurrected life to come. Perhaps we will be able to exercise new and remarkable abilities and do such things as the Lord Jesus did in His glorified body, such as when He passed through material objects, appeared and disappeared at various locations at will, and so forth.

Regardless of the many wonderful qualities and abilities that the resurrected bodies of the redeemed may possess, the greatest glory and joy of the Resurrection will be the capacity to behold the presence of God for all eternity, and not just with our spiritual senses but with our very own eyes: "For I know that my Redeemer lives, and at last he will stand upon the earth; and after my skin has been thus destroyed, then from my flesh I shall see God, whom I shall see on my side, and my eyes shall behold, and not another" (*Job* 19:25–26). This glorious sight will take place in the new Heaven and earth that will be formed following the General Resurrection. In the Book of Revelation, St. John describes it thus: "The holy city, new Jerusalem, coming down out of heaven from God, prepared as a bride adorned for her husband; and I heard a loud voice from the throne saying, 'Behold, the dwelling of God is with men. He will dwell with them, and they shall be his people, and God himself will be with them; he will wipe away every tear from their eyes, and death shall be no more, neither shall there be mourning nor crying nor pain any more, for the former things have passed away'" (*Rev.* 21:2–4). This seems to propose that the resurrected redeemed will live on earth, the new and transformed earth, and there enjoy the eternal vision of God. It also would seem that the wonderful spiritual qualities that we now associate with Heaven will then somehow be joined with the material but transfigured earth in a way that is glorious, astounding, and beyond our ability to presently comprehend. The effects that sin, death, and the devil have had on the earth—and indeed the entire universe—will be removed. One might very well expect that the familiar plants and animals and other aspects of creation that we now enjoy will also be redeemed and renewed and will be part of this new earth. Such a prospect is echoed in the vision of the peaceable kingdom from the Book of the Prophet Isaiah:

The wolf shall dwell with the lamb, and the leopard shall lie down with the kid, and the calf and the lion and the fatling together, and a little child shall lead them. The cow and the bear shall feed; their young shall lie down together; and the lion shall eat straw like the ox. The sucking child shall play over the hole of the asp, and the weaned child shall put his hand on the adder's den. They shall not hurt or destroy in all my holy mountain; for the earth shall be

full of the knowledge of the LORD as the waters cover the
sea. (*Is.* 11:6–9)

Such a transformation of nature appears to be what the resurrected blessed are meant to experience. As the *Catechism* says,
"The visible universe, then, is itself destined to be transformed,
'so that the world itself, restored to its original state, facing no
further obstacles, should be at the service of the just,' sharing
their glorification in the risen Jesus Christ."[1]

This, then, is the glorious consummation of all things that
the righteous are destined to share in and enjoy forever. But lest
we are tempted to presume upon this grace or become compla-
cent, we should remember that the righteous are not the only
ones who will be raised from the dead. The unjust will be raised
as well, but not to glory. Rather, they are raised to everlasting
shame and condemnation: "The resurrection of all the dead, 'of
both the just and the unjust,' will precede the Last Judgment.
This will be 'the hour when all who are in the tombs will hear
(the Son of Man's) voice and come forth, those who have done
good, to the resurrection of life, and those who have done evil,
to the resurrection of judgment."[2]

The resurrection of the unjust is a horrible thing to
contemplate, for in that resurrection to judgment and condemnation their bodies and souls will be reunited and will be
incorruptible in a manner similar to the just, but not to live forever blessedly with God in the new Heaven and earth. Instead,
they will live eternally separated from God in Hell and subject
to all manner of pain, suffering, and regret. The *Catechism* says,
"To die in mortal sin without repenting and accepting God's

---

1   *CCC*, 1047, 296.
2   *CCC*, 1038, 293.

merciful love means remaining separated from him forever by our own free choice. This state of definitive self-exclusion from communion with God and the blessed is called 'hell.'"[3] Even while contemplating the joys of the resurrection for the righteous dead, the reality of the resurrection of the unjust should encourage us ever more devoutly to live in faith, hope, and charity and to fervently seek God's help that we might conclude our time on this earth in a state of grace and friendship with Him.

---

3   CCC, 1033, 292.

Day 55

And the Word became flesh and dwelt among us, full of grace and truth; we have beheld his glory, glory as of the only Son from the Father.

         —*John* 1:14

The body (of Jesus) that lay lifeless in the tomb is ours. The body that rose again on the third day is ours. The body that ascended above all the heights of heaven to the right hand of the Father's glory is ours. If then we walk in the way of his command-ments, and are not ashamed to acknowledge the price he paid for our salvation in a lowly body, we too are to rise to share his glory. The promise he made will be fulfilled in the sight of all: "Whoever acknowledges me before men, I too will acknowledge him before my Father who is in heaven."   —Pope St. Leo the Great

Dear St. Leo, so many centuries have passed by since you wrote those words, yet we still have a similar problem: to believe that the soul can be saved but doubt that the body can! If we were founding a religion, we might be inclined to make it only about souls. We would think that an all-spiritual God would make only souls with a shimmering veil around them, never bodies that on earth can seem so gross. Part of what is called the mystery of the Incarnation is that the Son of God did come in the flesh to experience much of what we do. And since it was in this flesh that He promised us glorified bodies, let us receive this Good News not with doubt but with delighted faith. Amen.

Day 56

And night shall be no more; they need no light of lamp or sun, for the Lord God will be their light, and they shall reign forever and ever.   —Rev. 22:5

He showed me the robe which the bridegroom shows to the bride he has loved for so long. This robe was neither of purple, nor of scarlet, nor of sandal, nor of samite, but of some marvelous light which clothed her soul.   —Bl. Angela of Foligno

Jesus, we marvel that You would bother to show such things to Your poor little creature, Angela, on her deathbed. Yet, as the Saviour of our bodies as well as our souls, You seem to understand how much we need such images to take heart, especially toward the end of our time on earth. The demons try to tell us that Heaven is no more real than the tooth fairy. Failing that strategy, they tell us that Heaven will be as boring as sitting in a white room without windows. Using whatever image will horrify us, they try to lead us to indulge in the greatest pleasure possible in the last years of our lives. To penitential Saints, such as Angela of Foligno, You sometimes give lavish images of the physical glories of Heaven. Help us to persevere until the end in works of love, easy and hard, for our reward passes all understanding. Amen.

Day 57

Until we all attain to the unity of the faith and of the knowledge of the Son of God, to mature manhood, to the measure of the stature of the fullness of Christ.   —*Eph.* 4:13

"The works of God are perfect" (Deut. 32:4). But the resurrection will be the work of God. Therefore man will be remade perfect in all his members, just as the work of an art would not be perfect, if its product lacked any of the things contained in the art, so neither could man be perfect, unless the whole that is contained enfolded in the soul be outwardly unfolded in the body.

—St. Thomas Aquinas

Father God, some of us dislike our bodies because of the pain they cause us, or because they are not as beautiful as the bodies of others we admire. We may think it would be better if in Heaven we had only souls. Help us to believe that we will one day in Heaven have beautiful, perfect bodies that show forth the beauty of our redeemed souls. Help us to imagine how each of our resurrected bodies might look, brightly shining, without blemish and without the slightest suffering. Amen.

Day 58

[He] will change our lowly body to be like His glorious body,
by the power which enables Him even to subject all things to
Himself.   —*Phil.* 3:21

Whatever enters into the constitution of the human body
will rise again with it. Further, our resurrection will be conformed
to the resurrection of Christ. Now in Christ's resurrection His
blood rose again, else the wine would not now be changed into His
blood in the Sacrament of the altar.   —St. Thomas Aquinas

Come, Holy Spirit, enlighten our imaginations. Perhaps because of paintings of flimsily dressed cherubs we sometimes imagine that our resurrected bodies will be bloodless wraiths! True, the resurrected body of Jesus went through a closed door. However, doubting Thomas was able to stick his hand into the bloody wound in the side of Jesus. What might You, Holy Spirit, want us to think about our resurrected bodies when our images seem to conflict? I seem to hear You suggesting that what is important is that we understand our resurrected bodies will be flesh and blood, so help us stay away from any sad and erroneous thought that we shall be like ghosts. Amen.

Day 59

It is sown in weakness, it shall rise in power. —1 Cor. 15:43

Now Christ rose again of youthful age, which begins about the age of thirty years, as Augustine says. Therefore others also will rise again of a youthful age. God founded human nature without a defect; even so will He restore it without defect. Now human nature has a twofold defect. First, because it has not yet attained to its ultimate perfection. Secondly, because it has already gone back from its ultimate perfection. The first defect is found in children, the second in the aged: and consequently in each of these human nature will be brought by the resurrection to the state of its ultimate perfection which is in the youthful age, at which the movement of growth terminates, and from which the movement of decrease begins. —St. Thomas Aquinas

St. Thomas, something in the heart of humans leaps with joy at the thought of eternal youth in Heaven. In the book of Genesis, we are given an image of Adam and Eve before the Fall as what we would call today "young adults." Tradition teaches us that the wrinkles, failing organs, and other symptoms of aging came as part of the punishment for the Fall. It follows that the redeemed body in Heaven would be radiant with youthful power and beauty. For those of us who are old, suffering with the results of aging, your words, St. Thomas, come as music to our ears. Intercede for us that we may accept the trials of aging, but let us take heart at the thought of the renewal of our bodies in the Resurrection. Amen.

Day 60

And we shall be changed.   —*1 Cor.* 15:52

It is written: "It is sown in weakness, it shall rise in power," . . . *"mobile and living."* . . . *agility in movement. Therefore the glorified bodies will be agile. Slowness of movement would seem especially inconsistent with the nature of a spirit. The glorified body will be altogether subject to the glorified soul, so that there be nothing in it to resist the will of the spirit.*   —St. Thomas Aquinas

Father God, how much we love to watch things that move swiftly, from lightning and gazelles to runners and racing cars. We love to be agile and hate being forced to be sluggish. We feel oppressed when we cannot translate the desire of our will into an immediate bodily response—as when we are too crippled to even walk across a room. Come, speedily, to fill our minds with images of our own bodies fleet as that of a race horse or a dancer. May footsteps in the path of love now on earth lead us one day to lightning-speed fulfillment of Your holy will in Heaven. Amen.

Day 61

Then the righteous shall shine as the sun in the kingdom of their Father.   *—Matt.* 13:43

The bodies of the saints will be lightsome. Thus in the glorified body the glory of the soul will be known, even as through a crystal is known the color of a body contained in a crystal vessel. Thus we see bodies which have color by their nature aglow with the resplendence of the sun.   —St. Thomas Aquinas

Our Lady, great artists portray you in such a way that we can see the light of your spirit pouring through your face, your hands, and your gown. Those who see apparitions of you claim that no artist can come close to the resplendent glorious beauty of the image they saw. Even in our own lives, sometimes the love coming from the heart of other people fills their eyes with glowing light. But the desire to be beautiful or to be loved by a beautiful person can become an obsession for us. Mother Mary, turn our thoughts beyond mirrors and popular "stars" to the thought of the luminous beauty of you and Jesus, the Angels, and the Saints. Help us believe that if we let the Holy Spirit transform us into Saints, we, too, will one day have flawless souls, overflowing into bodies full of light. Amen.

Day 62

Come, spouse of Christ, receive the crown the Lord has prepared for you from all eternity.

—"Common of Virgins,"
Evening Prayer II, *Divine Office*

For a crown signifies some kind of perfection, on account of its circular shape, so that for this very reason it is becoming to the perfection of the blessed. The glory of the body is added to the beatitude of the soul, wherefore this same glory of the body is sometimes called an aureole. An aureole denotes a kind of joy in the works one has done, in that they have the character of a victory.

—St. Thomas Aquinas

Beautiful Saints in Heaven, we salute you in prayer. How often have we seen crowns and halos around your heads in works of art painted through the centuries! To daydream about having a crown or halo around our own heads while we are on earth would seem the height of presumption and vain glory. But after all our labors for the Kingdom, why should we not rejoice in the hope that one day our weary heads will be so crowned in Heaven? All Saints, intercede for us now that, indeed, grace will crown our feeble works. Amen.

Day 63

A hair of your head shall not perish.   —*Luke* 21:18

Further, hair and nails were given as an ornament. Now (our) bodies, especially of the elect, ought to rise again with all their adornment. Therefore they ought to rise again with the hair.
          —St. Thomas Aquinas

St. Thomas, in your writings you emphasized the wonder of God's creation. Before the Fall, hair and nails weren't associated with perms, dye, and nail polish. Intercede for us that images of naturally beautiful hair and nails as they will be in Heaven may delight us now, especially those of us who in our elderly years no longer love our hair and nails as we did when we were younger. Amen.

Day 64

Now this wise virgin has gone to Christ. Among the choirs of virgins, she is radiant as the sun in the heavens.
—Divine Office, "Feast of St. Scholastica"

When we rise again with glorious bodies, in the power of the Lord, these bodies will be white and resplendent as the snow, more brilliant than the sun, more transparent than crystal, and each one will have a special mark of honor and glory, according to the support and endurance of torments and sufferings, willingly and freely borne to the honor of God.   —Bl. Jan Van Ruysbroeck

Come Holy Spirit, help us to understand this vision of your mystic Saint, Blessed Jan Van Ruysbroeck. A special mark? Why not? Some of us choose, rightly or wrongly, to place an indelible tattoo on our bodies to symbolize some precious word or design. We firmly believe that we shall see the marks of the crown of thorns and the nails in Christ's resurrected body. Along with the glorious brightness Blessed Jan describes, let us look forward to some individual emblem that will signify the sacrifices we have willingly undertaken out of love for Jesus. Amen.

Day 65

As was man of dust, so are those who are of the dust; and as is the man of heaven, so are those who are of heaven. Just as we have borne the image of the man of dust, we shall also bear the image of the man of heaven.   —*1 Cor.* 15:48–49

As for our bodies, they shall be of most comely and gracious features; beauteous and lovely; healthful, without any weakness; always in youth, and in flower and prime of their force; personable in shape, as swift as our thought, incapable of grief, as clear as crystal, as bright as the sun, and as able to find passage through heaven, earth, or any other material impediment, as in the liquid and yielding air.   —St. Robert Southwell

God, Our Father, as we read St. Robert's description we are reminded of the Paradise You set us in at the beginning, the one that Adam and Eve lost. We love it when we can see the beautiful bodies of babies, children, and adults. We love to perform graceful movements or to succeed in sports. We love to watch others displaying their bodies to perfection: the leap of a dancer into the air or the plunge of a diver. Help us to savor such glimpses now of the future that You wish each of us to experience someday in eternity. Amen.

Day 66

It is sown in corruption, it shall rise in incorruption.

—1 Cor. 15:42

When God called Himself the God of Abraham, Isaac, and Jacob, He implied that those holy patriarchs were still alive, though they were no more seen on earth. Our Blessed Lord seems to tell us, that in some sense or other Abraham's body might be considered still alive as a pledge of his resurrection, though it was dead in the common sense in which we apply the word. His announcement is, Abraham shall rise from the dead, because in truth, he is still alive. He cannot in the end be held under the power of the grave, more than a sleeping man can be kept from waking. Abraham is still alive in the dust, though not risen thence. He is alive because all God's saints live to Him, though they seem to perish.

—Bl. John Henry Cardinal Newman

Blessed Cardinal Newman, your words puzzle us. "Mystery! Mystery! Mystery!" we are admonished when we try to understand the status of the body in eternity prior to the Judgment Day when all bodies will be resurrected. Some theologians write of some sort of "spiritual" body that will be ours in Purgatory. This might explain all the visions of physical happenings in Purgatory. Now that you know all about it from your heavenly place, help us not to strain for clarity now but to wait in faith, open to whatever glimpses of these mysteries the Holy Spirit might wish to bestow on us. Amen.

Day 67

For the moment all discipline seems painful rather than pleasant; later it yields the peaceful fruit of righteousness to those who have been trained by it.   —Heb. 12:11

As a matter of fact, it's no great convenience to be composed of a body and a soul! Miserable Brother Ass, as St. Francis of Assisi called the body, often hinders his noble sister and prevents her from darting off where she would. Still, I won't abuse him, for all his faults; he is still good for something, he helps his companion to get to heaven, and gets there himself.   —St. Thérèse of Lisieux

St. Thérèse, Doctor of the Church, you taught us about the body's helping us get to Heaven by your saintly acceptance of the painful crosses of tuberculosis. We usually think more of the soul being rewarded in Heaven than of the body, but surely the joys of our resurrected bodies will far outweigh all our physical sufferings on earth, no matter how dreadful. Please send us graces to endure the small and much larger pains our bodies have to endure at this time of our lives. Amen.

SAINT VERONICA

6

In Heaven, We Will Do
Wonderful Things

When discussing the subject of Heaven it is not uncommon to hear some people, especially young persons, wonder if Heaven might actually be boring. Such is not surprising, really, when one comes to understand the typical expectations that many people have about Heaven. Some view Heaven as a wispy, ethereal place where the only activity of its inhabitants consists of sitting around on clouds for all eternity in long white robes while plucking on harps and chanting. It isn't difficult to see how this scenario would fail to appeal to a lot of people!

In contemporary society, especially in the technologically advanced world of North American culture, people have been conditioned to have short attention spans. Modern humanity experiences an ever-increasing exposure to brief media sound bites, the expectation of instant gratification in all areas of life from communication to information gathering and fast food, along with an almost insatiable need for constant sensory stimulation and entertainment. When this present-day reality is taken into consideration, then the fear of boredom in the life to come becomes more understandable. This is especially so when one has an erroneous view of Heaven to begin with. If one's image of Heaven pictures a boring reality, then the problem is with the image, not with Heaven.

Let me put this as plainly as possible: Heaven will not be boring! The basic reason that this is so has little to do with the variety of activities that the righteous souls will undertake (though they may be many) and everything to do with the relationship they will experience in a particular singularity. And that experience is precisely this: they will behold God face-to-face in the Beatific Vision.[1]

God is the fullness of being. He is infinite. He is the source of limitless wisdom, knowledge, and understanding. He is the source of being itself. And because all this, and much more, is true, our contemplation of Him in the Beatific Vision also will be limitless and infinite. In this contemplation we will experience the utmost happiness that is humanly possible and will be perfectly fulfilled and contented, and even excited, at the unfathomable vistas that are opened to us in the presence of God. So for this reason alone, Heaven will not be boring.

That being said, it does not follow that we will have no activities to undertake in Heaven. The Scripture provides many images that assist us in thinking about what Heaven might be like. They liken it to guests having a good time at a great wedding banquet (*Rev.* 19:7–10); they speak of enjoying fine wine and scrumptious food in the Kingdom of God (*Is.* 25:6); they mention that new songs will be composed and sung there (*Rev.* 5:9; 14:3); they speak of a large and beautiful city just waiting to be explored (*Heb.* 11:16; 13:14; *Rev.* 20:2, 10–22); they state that the faithful servants of our Lord will be put in charge of many things and have numerous duties (*Matt.* 25:21, 23). In Heaven the righteous souls are seen as reigning with Christ, which

---

1 CCC, 1045, 295.

implies having great responsibilities (*Rev.* 25:5). The redeemed in Heaven are understood to be in mutual communion in an intimate and perfect relationship with God, the Angels, and other redeemed souls. Imagine the wonderful conversations and discussions that will take place there! And for those nature lovers and gardeners who like to till the soil and work with foliage, another image of fulfillment in the Kingdom of God is that of abundant vegetation and verdant plantings (*Is.* 35). All this suggests that life in the Kingdom will be busy and active.

Exactly how all this might be realized is not fully understood. Since the character of Heaven before the General Resurrection is that of a spiritual state of existence for the righteous who await the reunion of their bodies and souls, we might more easily think of these activities as being part of the resurrected life in the new Heaven and earth. Regardless, however it comes to pass we can be sure that it will be interesting, enjoyable, fulfilling, and far from boring.

Day 68

In Jesus Christ, our Lord and King, we are already seated at your right hand. We look forward to praising you in the fellowship of all your saints in our heavenly homeland.

—*Liturgy of the Hours*, "Sunday Evening Prayer II," Week IV

Let us sing alleluia here on earth, while we still live in anxiety, so that we may sing it one day in heaven in full security.

—St. Augustine

St. Augustine, we know you loved to sing, for you tell us that your holy mother, St. Monica, upbraided you for singing chants of praise even in the privy! We read your insight and understand; here on earth, our alleluias are not totally full since they are accompanied by our fears. Since all will be redeemed and glorified in Heaven, even those of us who don't sing well will be able to harmonize with all the Angels and Saints in our praises. Help us to smile in the midst of our fear, because of the gift of hope. Amen.

Day 69

And now give thanks to God, for I am ascending to him who sent me.   *—Tob.* 12:20

The glorified bodies are moved sometimes, since even Christ's body was moved in His Ascension. It is likely that they will sometimes move according as it pleases them, that their vision may be refreshed by the beauty of the variety of creatures. And yet movement will nowise diminish their happiness which consists in seeing God, for He will be everywhere present to them.

—St. Thomas Aquinas

Holy Spirit, You know everything, and so You surely know that there are some Christians who don't look forward to Heaven because they think of it as some kind of "frozen glory" without any of the joys we experience on earth. But Scripture and Tradition teach us that in our resurrected bodies we will move swiftly. Yet this will not diminish our experience of the Trinity. A child has fun romping about while ever aware of the presence of his smiling parent. Like an Olympic gymnast flexing his muscles before the leap onto the bar, let us now rejoice in the motions of our bodies as we await the leap on the Last Day. Amen.

Day 70

And in the Spirit he carried me away to a great, high mountain, and showed me the holy city Jerusalem coming down out of heaven from God, having the glory of God, its radiance like a most rare jewel, like a jasper, clear as crystal.   —Rev. 21:10–11

Our sight shall feed on the most glorious majesty of the place, and on the glory and beauty of the company; the ear shall always be solaced with the sweet and angelical harmony; in fine, every sense shall have its several and peculiar delight. There plenty cloys not; there, gaiety offends not; there hunger is satisfied, yet not diminished.   —St. Robert Southwell

Holy Spirit, what an antidote these words of your Saint are to the fear some of us have that Heaven will be boring. Is it because sins of the flesh are associated with sensuality that we fail to understand that our senses were originally made for God-willed delight? As we read this passage from St. Robert, help us to think of gifts already given: of majestic natural beauty, sublime music, or well-prepared banquets. On earth none of these can totally satisfy our desire for total bliss, for our bodies bring weariness even in the midst of splendor, but in Heaven . . . oh, help us believe that these gifts will be without end. Amen.

Day 71

He brought me to the banqueting house, and his banner over
me was love.   —*Sg.* 2:4

In heaven we shall be as the angels of God; we shall nei-
ther marry, nor be married, nor shall we stand in need of food to
support life. The supper therefore will consist of spiritual riches,
and delights, and glory, and ornament, suitable to the state of the
blessed. Riches and delights are mentioned in this life, because we
see not things more excellent. But from these we may learn, that the
spiritual supper will be so superior to our most splendid banquets,
as heaven is to earth, and as God who will prepare it, is above all
mortals in power and majesty.   —St. Robert Bellarmine

Holy Spirit, since You have not chosen to teach us through
the Magisterium of the Church whether we shall eat in the manner we know or, instead, in some manner we cannot imagine,
we read such excerpts from the Saints with a grain of salt! What
they all agree on, however, is that we will feel totally fulfilled in
our bodies, souls, hearts, and minds. What comes to mind is the
folly of a woman enjoying the first kiss of a beloved man and
complaining that she can't eat a piece of candy at the same time!
Help us to let these heavenly pleasures remain in the area of
mystery so that we may add surprise to our contentment. Amen.

Day 72

Therefore, since we are surrounded by so great a cloud of witnesses, let us also lay aside every weight, and sin which clings so closely, and let us run with perseverance the race that is set before us.   —Heb. 12:1

I feel that I am about to enter into my rest. But I feel especially that my mission is about to begin, my mission to make God loved as I love him, to give my little way to souls. If God grants my desires, my heaven will be spent on earth until the end of time. Yes, I want to spend my heaven doing good on earth. This isn't impossible, since from the bosom of the Beatific Vision, the angels watch over us. I can't make heaven a feast of rejoicing. I can't rest as long as there are souls to be saved. But when the angel says; 'Time is no more!' then I will take my rest. I will be able to rejoice, because the number of the elect will be complete, and because all will have entered into joy and repose. My hearts beats with joy at this thought.   —St. Thérèse of Lisieux

Dear St. Thérèse, when most of us read those words of yours for the first time, we are astounded. Yet you would not have been canonized if those words were considered by our Church authorities to be sentimental idiocy. Therefore, we make bold to pray that we may experience your personal intercession powerfully, especially in what concerns our own salvation and that of those we fear for. Amen.

Day 73

All have sinned and fall short of the glory of God.

—*Rom.* 3:23

I believe the Blessed in Heaven have great compassion for our miseries. They remember that when they were weak and mortal like us, they committed the same faults themselves and went through the same struggles, and their fraternal tenderness becomes still greater than it ever was on earth. It's on account of this that they never stop watching over us and praying for us.

—St. Thérèse of Lisieux

Dear Mother Mary, when you were on earth you had in you no sin. This did not stop you from loving sinners! In fact you could love them more than we do. I think our love for other sinners is sometimes mixed up with secret envy of the sins they seem to get away with. On the other hand, often we feel we cannot love them because their sins victimize us and others we care about. How grateful we will be in Purgatory for the prayers of those who have already reached the goal, some of whom were our victims! How happy we will be in Heaven when we can express our love for sinners with purity of heart in simple compassion! Amen.

7

Preparing for Heaven

In the Psalms, we read a prayer beseeching the Almighty to "teach us to number our days that we may get a heart of wisdom" (*Ps.* 90:12). Every Christian who longs to make Heaven their eternal destiny would do well to heed this counsel, for the first step in fulfilling that desire is to be mindful of one's own mortality. In order to prepare for Heaven, it is necessary to number one's days and realize that they are indeed limited: "As for man, his days are like grass; he flourishes like a flower of the field; for the wind passes over it, and it is gone, and its place knows it no more" (*Ps.* 103:15–16).

Unless the Lord hastens his coming with the consummation of the age, every person conceived, every person reading these very words, will one day die. That is not, however, the kind of meditation that finds great popularity in our day, an era that seems utterly dedicated to the maintenance of health, youth, and death-denying vigor, or, if those cannot be procured, to at least the appearance of such. But the fact remains that ultimately, for all people, the mortality rate is 100 percent. Some of us will die young and tragically, others will die old and full of years; all of us, however, will die. So if we are to prepare for Heaven we must prepare for death and, hopefully, a good death.

What does it mean to have a good death? Each individual would probably have his own ideas and opinions in answer to this question. Many would say that a good death would be one that is peaceful and devoid of physical pain or suffering. Others might say that it would be one in which the dying person has control over the circumstances: the location, his medical or palliative care, the loved ones present, the fate of his body and possessions following death, and other details and concerns. All of these, and more, might constitute what society at large would consider a good death.

The Catholic Church, however, while accepting or accommodating many of these particular temporal matters, has always understood a good death to mean specifically one in which a person dies in the state of grace in the friendship of God, free from the condemnation of mortal sin. Catholics understand this consolation to be the most important issue as one approaches the end of life and that such a death is not to be feared since it is the means by which the soul will be brought into the nearer presence of God to behold and enjoy forever the Beatific Vision. In such a circumstance, death is not the final word and is not ultimately a "real" death at all.

There is, however, what the Church understands as a true, real, and everlasting death. As Pope Benedict XVI has taught, "the authentic death, which one must fear, is that of the soul, called by the Book of Revelation, 'second death' (*Rev.* 20:14–15; 21:8). In fact, he who dies in mortal sin, without repentance, locked in prideful rejection of God's love, excludes himself from the Kingdom of life."[1] This death, the death of eternal damnation in Hell, is one that a Christian stridently seeks to avoid through a life of earnest preparation for Heaven. The Church

---

1   Pope Benedict XVI, Angelus message, November 6, 2006.

teaches that immediately after death, the soul of every individual faces its own particular judgment at which instant its eternal destination will be revealed and established: "Each man receives his eternal retribution in his immortal soul at the very moment of his death, in a particular judgment that refers his life to Christ: either entrance into the blessedness of heaven— through a purification or immediately,—or immediate and everlasting damnation."[2]

In order to be ready to face with hope one's own particular judgment at the hour of death, it is helpful—even essential—to prepare for that eventuality by having frequent recourse to the Sacrament of Confession. Just as the Jewish Temple was cleansed during the earthly ministry of our Lord,(John 2:12–25) so must the temples of our bodies and souls be cleansed during our lifetimes if we are to be made ready to meet our Saviour at his coming or at our death. Many of the writers and Fathers of the early Church (e.g., Origen, St. Irenaeus, St. Augustine) understood the account of the cleansing of the temple to symbolically represent, at one level, our souls and bodies, the dwelling place of the Holy Spirit wherein nothing unclean or unlawful should find an abode. The icon of the Cleansing of the Temple that accompanies this chapter depicts our Lord driving out all alien things from the Temple of his Father. In a similar fashion, we should be zealous in our own lives about ridding ourselves of any and all things that are contrary to the will of our Lord.

This is accomplished in the first instance through the Sacrament of Confession. Because of the frailty and flaws of human nature, this Sacrament, also known as Penance or the Sacrament of Reconciliation, was given by our Lord to the Church in order that serious sins committed after Baptism could be forgiven and

---

2   *CCC*, 1022, 368.

sinners reconciled with God and his Church. Jesus said [to his Apostles], "Peace be with you. As the Father has sent me, even so I send you" (*John* 20:21 RSV-CE). And when he had said this, he breathed on them and said, "Receive the Holy Spirit. If you forgive the sins of any, they are forgiven; if you retain the sins of any, they are retained" (*John* 20:21–23). Through apostolic succession, the apostles passed down this power to forgive sins to the bishops and priests of the Church who exercise it in the name and stead of Christ. All Catholics who have reached the age of reason are required by the law of the Church to confess at least once per year all the grave sins they may have committed since their last confession. This is, of course, a minimal requirement, and the Church strongly recommends frequent use of this Sacrament. In particular, those who are serious about growing in holiness and preparing themselves to enter Heaven will go to Confession regularly.

The most fruitful use of the Sacrament will include beforehand a careful examination of one's conscience in order to honestly and truthfully assess the state of one's soul in relation to God. One of the best ways to do this is to think about the quality of one's life, and the sins one may have committed, in light of the Ten Commandments. A good example of such an examination of conscience is included in Appendix E. Also, piously and prayerfully meditating upon the Word of God in Sacred Scripture is an invaluable source of spiritual nourishment and enlightenment, revealing to us God's will as well as the condition of our relationship with him: "Thy word is a lamp to my feet and a light to my path" (*Ps.* 119:105). Those who approach Confession with sincere sorrow for their sins and with a firm purpose of amending their life and doing acts of penance and reparation toward repairing the damage done by their sin, receive not only the grace of forgiveness and reconciliation with

God and the Church but many other salutary spiritual benefits as well. The absolved penitent obtains peace and consolation of mind and heart, as well as the grace needed to avoid sin in the future, and increased holiness and sanctification of life.

Closely related to the Sacrament of Confession, and understood to be an integral part of the necessary acts of the penitent done in and through Christ, is the performance of penance and good works as satisfaction for one's sins. The *Catechism* tells us that these acts "can consist of prayer, an offering, works of mercy, service of neighbor, voluntary self-denial, sacrifices, and above all the patient acceptance of the cross we must bear. Such penances help configure us to Christ, who alone expiated our sins once for all. They allow us to become co-heirs with the risen Christ, 'provided we suffer with him.'"[3]

When we perform these works in faith, obedience, and trust, we are joined more and more to the person and work of Christ as we cooperate with him in "work[ing] out [our] own salvation with fear and trembling" (*Phil.* 2:12). In fact, the entire fabric of our day-to-day lives should be contoured and characterized by the self-sacrificial love of the Saviour whom we seek to emulate. This becomes especially important in the context of preparing for Heaven if we are experiencing suffering or other trials that frequently beset us in this life. In such circumstances we are called to accept our difficulties and spiritually join our sufferings, our challenges, our burdens, and our sorrows to the Cross of Christ. In this way, as we imitate Christ and, by an act of our will aided by divine grace, intentionally configure our trials to those of His Passion, our suffering becomes redemptive. It can be "offered up" to the Lord for the intention of our

---

3   *CCC*, 1460, 407.

own continued conversion, sanctification, and final salvation, for that of others, or for some other good and worthy purpose.

Doing so allows us to sacrificially offer our suffering for a greater good, placing it within an ultimately meaningful context. This frees us from being a mere victim of pain or disability by empowering us to direct our suffering purposefully and use it positively. Thus joined to Christ's own sacrificial suffering in His Passion and death, we participate in some small way in the redemption of the world—and thus in our own redemption—by identifying with and joining our sufferings to the ultimate suffering of the Crucified One. Doing so, as St. Paul reminds us, "in [our] flesh [we] complete what is lacking in Christ's afflictions for the sake of his Body, that is, the Church" (*Col.* 1:24). In this way, as we cooperate with our Lord's own greater sacrifice for the world, nothing is wasted, not even our suffering, but everything is used by God in the process of our redemption and in the whole economy of salvation.

Directly linked with sacrificial actions such as these is the opportunity that the Church provides for obtaining sanctification through receiving indulgences from the treasury of merit gained by Christ and the Saints. The *Catechism* teaches that an indulgence is "the remission before God of the temporal punishment due to sin whose guilt has already been forgiven. A properly disposed member of the Christian faithful can obtain an indulgence under prescribed conditions through the help of the Church which, as the minister of redemption, dispenses and applies with authority the treasury of the satisfactions of Christ and the saints."[4] There are numerous ways that an indulgence can be gained. The *Handbook of Indulgences: Norms and Grants* lists over seventy indulgenced acts and good works that the faithful

---

4   *CCC*, 1471, 411.

can perform on behalf of themselves or for the departed. Doing these indulgenced good works in faith and hope can bring great consolation in that not only are we cooperating in the Lord's sanctification of ourselves and the world but, being assisted by God's grace, we may even be given the gift of shortening our experience of Purgatory, or perhaps avoiding it altogether by being ushered into the Divine Presence immediately following our death. This is a great mercy devoutly to be hoped for and striven for by all who seek to prepare themselves for Heaven.

Another invaluable resource that is made available to us as we prepare for Heaven is the Sacrament of the Anointing of the Sick. Because of the name by which this Sacrament was formerly known (Extreme Unction), it is frequently thought that a person must be at the point of death (*in extremis*) before he can receive it, but this is not the case. Many who read this book may suffer from illnesses or conditions that are life threatening, may be facing a serious surgical procedure, or may be approaching death from the frailty of old age itself. If any of these circumstances are present, it is appropriate to receive this Sacrament. Even if someone currently does not struggle with these grave conditions, it is likely that they will at some future point. At such occasions, it is very important to receive this holy anointing because of the great benefits it confers. Among those benefits are the following:

- The uniting of the sick person to the Passion of Christ, for his own good and that of the whole Church
- The strengthening, peace, and courage to endure in a Christian manner the sufferings of illness or old age
- The forgiveness of sins, if the sick person was not able to obtain it through the Sacrament of Penance

- The restoration of health, if it is conducive to the salvation of his soul
- The preparation for passing over to eternal life

We should not wait until we feel that we are near death to send for a priest to confer this Sacrament. Rather, as soon as circumstances arise that make the Anointing of the Sick appropriate, a priest should be called so that there can be a full and conscious participation of the sick person in the liturgical actions of the Sacrament.

All that has been said thus far in this chapter has assumed an active life of prayer on the part of the one who desires to prepare for Heaven. That is essential. Quite simply, as St. John Damascene tells us, "Prayer is the raising of one's mind and heart to God." Prayer can take many forms and have varied content. Prayer can embrace blessing, adoration, petition, intercession, thanksgiving, and praise. It can take the form of liturgical prayer, such as in the Daily Office of the Church (also known as the Liturgy of the Hours), or through praying and meditating on the mysteries of the Rosary. There is an honored history among Catholics of venerating the Blessed Virgin Mary, and the prayers of the Rosary seeking her intercession as one meditates on the significant events of salvation history can be particularly effective in attaining genuine preparation for Heaven.

Similarly, the prayerful veneration of all the Saints as we ask for their intercession on our behalf is very helpful. Prayer can be also extemporaneous and unscripted. It can be vocal or silent, meditative or contemplative. Prayer is at once both a simple and a profound undertaking, but, regardless of its contours, it has as its purpose and end—a fundamental, individual communion with God. This communion embraces a relationship that is experienced personally between God and the baptized believer but also is experienced communally in and through the Church. Such a vital life of prayer is essential for anyone who seriously desires to embark on an earnest and sincere preparation for Heaven.

The highest and most perfect act of prayer, however, is to be found in the celebration of the Holy Sacrifice of the Mass. The Church teaches us that "the Eucharist contains and expresses all forms of prayer: it is 'the pure offering' of the whole Body of Christ to the glory of God's name, and according to the traditions of East and West, it is the 'sacrifice of praise.'"[5] In fact, everything that one does to prepare for Heaven—the Sacrament of Confession, penance, prayer, offerings, works of mercy, service of neighbor, self-denial, sacrifices, bearing the cross, the Sacrament of Anointing, and so forth—all of it is oriented toward and irrevocably joined to the celebration of the Mass. This is so because the Mass is "the source and summit of the Christian life."[6] In the Mass, we not only receive graces to help us prepare for Heaven; we receive Jesus himself, the One in whose friendship and presence we seek to live forever in the glories of paradise. In the Eucharist, under the outward forms of bread and wine, Jesus truly and substantially is present—His Body and Blood, His Soul and Divinity. In Holy Communion, our union with the Lord in this life is increased, even as we receive a pledge and foretaste of the heavenly feast that is to come.

Thus the Church teaches us that "by the Eucharistic celebration we already unite ourselves with the heavenly liturgy and anticipate eternal life, when God will be all in all."[7] The richness of the Holy Mass, the height and depth and breadth of meaning

---

5   *CCC*, 2643, 697.

6   *CCC*, 368.

7   *CCC*, 1326, 369.

and experience that it conveys, is inestimable. Suffice it to say that we who seek eternal life with God as the goal of our greatest longing and deepest happiness should frequently participate in this Holy Mystery, even beyond fulfilling the minimum of our Sunday and Holy Day obligations. One such laudable custom is assisting at daily Mass. We should welcome every opportunity to receive the Blessed Sacrament, remembering that, as St. Ignatius of Antioch put it, "it is the medicine of immortality and the antidote against death, enabling us to live forever in Jesus Christ."

Day 74

"For behold, henceforth all generations will call me blessed."
—*Luke* 1:48

He who is devout to the Virgin Mother will certainly never be lost.   —St. Ignatius of Antioch

Virgin Mother Mary, we love you. We thank you for your maternal protection for us. Often we pray your Rosary as if it were a spiritual lullaby to soothe us in our weariness and troubles. So many Saints had visions of your coming to help them as they neared death, the gateway to eternity. As we begin reading this chapter about preparing for Heaven, please let us constantly commend ourselves to your Immaculate Heart. Amen.

Day 75

Let my prayer be counted as incense before thee. —*Ps.* 141:2

Prayer is the wing wherewith the soul flies to heaven, and meditation the eye wherewith we see God.

—St. Ambrose of Milan

St. Ambrose, would you believe that there are Christians who don't really like praying? Some of us, as children, were bored by long prayers in church and never came to understand these prayers on a deeper level. Some of us have tried meditation techniques and found they left us tired rather than uplifted. Intercede for us that we may be open to ways of prayer suited to each of us personally. We beg the Holy Spirit to refresh our prayer so that it may become ever more strengthening. Amen.

Day 76

If we confess our sins, he is faithful and just, and will forgive our sins and cleanse us from all unrighteousness. —1 Jn. 1:9

God means to fill each of you with what is good; so cast out what is bad! If he wishes to fill you with honey and you are full of sour wine, where is the honey to go? The vessel must be emptied of its contents and then be cleansed. Yes, it must be cleansed even if you have to work hard and scour it. It must be made fit for the new thing, whatever it may be. We may go on speaking figuratively, but whatever we say we cannot express the reality we are to receive. The name of that reality is God. —St. Augustine

Jesus, our Lord, we thank you for giving us the Sacrament of Reconciliation so that each week, if we need it, we can be cleansed of our sins. As we grow older, help us to be humble enough to make use of this method of scrubbing our souls of everything bad in preparation for one day receiving into them the absolute goodness of God. Amen.

Day 77

Be sober, be watchful. Your adversary the devil prowls around like a roaring lion, seeking someone to devour.   —1 Ptr. 5:8

Allow me, brothers, to look toward heaven rather than at the earth, so that my spirit may set on the right course when the time comes for me to go on my journey to the Lord. [He sees the devil standing near.] "Why do you stand there, you bloodthirsty brute? Murderer, you will not have me for your pretty. Abraham is welcoming me into his embrace."   —St. Martin de Tours

St. Martin, hero of early Church times, converted soldier, we like the militancy of your rebuke of the devil! Sometimes we do let the demons play with our minds. At first we may find it intriguing to consider the possibility that we can just live out our lives on our own terms without fear of God. But eventually such ideas lead only to despair as we confront the crosses, small and huge, in our lives. At such times let us firmly rebuke the voice of the devil and think instead of Abraham and Jesus and all the Saints eager to embrace us in an eternity of victory. Amen.

Day 78

"If you forgive the sins of any, they are forgiven."

—*John* 20:23

Through the mystery of the water and blood flowing out from the Lord's side, the robber received the sprinkling that gave him the forgiveness of sins. "You will be with me in this garden of delights." —St. Ephraim of Syria

Jesus, help us to come to you no matter what our sin or shame so that we may receive the same forgiveness that the thief on the cross received. We long to hear those words that we will be with You forever. Knowing this deep need, You instituted the Sacrament of Reconciliation when You empowered the Apostles to forgive sins. Let us flee to the loving graces You want to give us through the sacrificial ministry of our priests. Amen.

Day 79

"Blessed are the pure in heart, for they shall see God."
　　　　　　　　　　　　　　　　　　　—*Matt.* 5:8

The blessedness of seeing God is justly promised to the pure of heart. For the eye that is unclean would not be able to see the brightness of the true light, and what would be happiness to clear minds would be a torment to those that are defiled. Therefore, let the mists of worldly vanities be dispelled, and the inner eye be cleansed of all the filth of wickedness, so that the soul's gaze may feast serenely upon the great vision of God.

　　　　　　　　　　　　　　　　—Pope St. Leo the Great

God the Father, we believe that You made Purgatory the place where those of us who love You but are still not Saints at the time of our death, could be made ready to see Your true light. We can shorten that time right now by detaching ourselves from every obstacle to holiness that remains in our souls. Let us come out of denial and humbly beg You to woo us out of our love for darkness and accustom our eyes to Your light. Amen.

Day 80

What does it profit, my brethren, if a man says he has faith but has not works? —Jas. 2:14

If you wish to take up your abode in the tabernacle of the heavenly kingdom, you must reach there through your good works, without which you cannot hope to enter. —St. Benedict

St. Benedict, your Rule has survived many centuries and has been pondered by lay people as well as religious. Help us see what good works the Holy Spirit inspires in us in our times: willing some of our savings or property to charitable institutions; smiling at those around us even when we are in pain; forgiving anyone who hurts us; or calling a sick or sad friend on the phone? When we join the stream of God's love for others by such deeds, we are surely expanding our hearts to be part of the heavenly kingdom. Amen.

Day 81

Whom have I in heaven but thee? And there is nothing upon earth that I desire besides thee. My flesh and my heart may fail, but God is the strength of my heart and my portion forever.

— Ps. 73:25–26

Rise from love of the world and love of pleasure. Put care aside, strip your mind, refuse your body. Prayer after all, is a turning away from the world, visible and invisible. What have I longed for on earth besides You? Nothing except simply to cling always to You in undistracted prayer. Wealth pleases some, glory others, possessions others, but what I want is to cling to God and to put the hopes in Him.   —St. John Climacus

St. John Climacus, spiritual master, we feel ashamed when we read your words. If it is not wealth that pleases us, it is often glory in the form of being thought well of by others or receiving specific treasured possessions! We know this is true because of the anxiety or anger we feel when they seem threatened. Yet in one moment God can stop our fears and rage and sweep us up into contemplation of Himself as our greatest good. Intercede for us that, like you, we may experience such joy in God whenever we are assailed by that anxiety or anger. Amen.

Day 82

"My yoke is easy, and my burden is light."   —Matt. 11:30

If you want to be certain of being in the number of the Elect, strive to be one of the few, not one of the many. And if you would be quite sure of your salvation, strive to be among the fewest of the few; that is to say: do not follow the great majority of mankind, but follow those who enter upon the narrow way, who renounce the world, who give themselves to prayer, and who never relax their efforts by day or night, so that they may attain everlasting blessedness.

—St. Anselm of Canterbury

Oh, St. Anselm, how trapped many of us are in the "everybody's doing it" syndrome! Instead of asking ourselves, "what would a Saint do now?," we sink into mediocrity. Why? Laziness, inertia, or, perhaps, the fear that if we ever gave our will over to God entirely He might ask from us more than we could stand to give? Yet the Saints teach us that what is terribly difficult to do alone is much lighter when we yoke ourselves to Jesus to do it with us. Come, Lord Jesus, show us how much lighter a burden could be with Your help, so we will forge ahead bravely. Amen.

Day 83

And when he heard that it was Jesus of Nazareth, he began to cry out and say, "Jesus, Son of David, have mercy on me!"

—*Mark* 10:47

Every time we look at the Blessed Sacrament our place in heaven is raised forever.

I will go to him gladly in whatever way he wants, whether my death be sudden or long foreseen, knowing that his mercy will not fail, for without it I cannot be saved, whether death is long foreseen or sudden.   —St. Gertrude

St. Gertrude, in our time, adoration of the Blessed Sacrament is more and more available to us in our churches. Because coming to Jesus in this way requires faith and sometimes a sacrifice of time, we can fail to take advantage of this chance to rush more swiftly toward Heaven. As believing Christians, should we not be ready whether death comes suddenly or after long, drawn-out illness? We protest that if we had lots of time we would be sure to make good use of it in doing penance, but you are telling us, St. Gertrude, that the most essential part of a good death is calling on the mercy of the Lord. One intense prayer for mercy may equal many prayers muttered by habit thoughtlessly. You love us, Jesus, and we are yours. Amen.

Day 84

And he answered them, "He who has two coats, let him share with him who has none; and he who has food, let him do likewise."
                                                    —*Luke* 3:11

Let us have charity and humility, and give alms, for almsgiving cleanses our souls from the filth of sin. At death we lose all that we have in this world, but we take with us charity and the alms deeds we have done, and for these we shall receive a great reward from God.   —St. Francis of Assisi

Oh, St. Francis, in your times no one balked when you referred to sin as filth. But many of us have become such experts in denial that we excuse even sins that can be mortal as if they were mere weaknesses not even worth confessing! We find in our stores a thousand remedies taking away different forms of dirt in our hair, our skin, our mouths, yet to go to the Sacrament of Reconciliation to remove the dirt of venial or mortal sin seems to us too difficult! St. Francis, preach in our hearts as you did when you lived on earth that we may wake up. Amen.

Day 85

He said, "In a certain city there was a judge who neither feared God nor regarded man; and there was a widow in that city who kept coming to him and saying, 'Vindicate me against my adversary.' For a while he refused; but afterward he said to himself, 'Though I neither fear God nor regard man, yet because this widow bothers me, I will vindicate her, or she will wear me out by her continual coming.'"

And the Lord said, "Hear what the unrighteous judge says. And will not God vindicate his elect, who cry to him day and night?"   —Luke 18:2–7

The soul cannot have true knowledge of God through its own efforts or by means of any created thing, but only by divine light and by a special gift of divine grace. I believe there is no quicker or easier way for the soul to obtain this divine grace from God, supreme Good and supreme Love, than by a devout, pure, humble, continual, and violent prayer.   —St. Angela of Foligno

St. Angela, you urge us to devout, pure, humble, and continual prayer. We readily see that we are enjoined to pray that way throughout the New Testament. But "violent"? We suppose, St. Angela, that what you mean is passionate begging of the Lord to help us when we feel weak and unable to cope with life in a virtuous manner. If we feel victimized by the faults and sins of others we can go into despair and feel abandoned even by God. St. Angela, vehement Italian woman Saint, teach us how to storm Heaven. Amen.

Day 86

"But he who endures to the end will be saved."

—*Matt.* 24:13

Yet I know well that in some tribulation there is such sore sickness or other grievous bodily pain that it would be hard for a man to say a long prayer. And yet some who lie dying say full devoutly the seven psalms and other prayers with the priest at their anointing. But those who for the grief of their pain cannot endure to do it, or who are more tender and lack that strong heart and stomach that some others have, God requireth no such long prayers of them. But the lifting up of their heart alone, without any words at all, is more acceptable to him from one in such a state, than long service so said as folk usually say it in health. The martyrs in their agony made no long prayers aloud, but one inch of such a prayer, so prayed in that pain, was worth more, even (than) their own prayers, prayed at some other time.

—St. Thomas More

Holy Spirit, what is it in our human nature that makes us think that worth is tied to quantity, as if ten little pecks would show more love than one strong kiss! Of course it is true that willingness to pray at length shows more love than praying only a little bit out of laziness. Yet so dismally does illness and pain twist our minds that many think they are offending God by not praying enough, when offering up their distress out of love for God shows greater love than longer prayers. We thank you, St. Thomas More, for your wisdom about this matter. Pray for us to have the filial trust in God you had so that our minds will be clear of crippling scruples. Amen.

Day 87

"Behold, he will slay me; I have no hope; yet I will defend my ways to his face."   —*Job* 13:15

God's way of dealing with those whom He intends to admit soonest after this life into the possession of His everlasting glory, is to purify them in this world by the greatest afflictions and trials.

—St. Ignatius of Loyola

St. Ignatius, what a hard saying! We wish instead that those most deserving of immediate entrance into Heaven would pass at least the last part of their lives in ecstatic delight. How like spoiled children we are! Yet psychologists tell us that, deep down, children understand that if they are coddled and never disciplined it is a sign not of love but of neglect. And we know that Olympic athletes reach victory only through long sacrifice. Since we cannot enter Heaven except by being cleansed, should we not be glad to let this happen on earth rather than even more intensely in Purgatory? Merciful Jesus, you understand how hard it is for us to bear the afflictions of life. Do not judge us harshly for begging to be relieved of heavy crosses, but help us to flee from complaint into valiant trust. Amen.

Day 88

For me to live is Christ, and to die is gain.   —*Phil.* 1:21

Death is ecstasy.
Remember that you have only one soul; that you have only one death to die; that you have only one life. If you do this, there will be many things about which you care nothing.

—St. Teresa of Avila

St. Teresa, Doctor of the Church, teach us to ask about everything that bothers or worries us. If I were to know I would die tomorrow, would a spot on my clothing concern me? A trivial mistake that made me look stupid? Loss of time because of waiting for someone who is late? In your most famous prayer you tell us not to let anything disturb us, since God alone is enough. Is it not proof that we believe that God is enough and that we are less anxious about small concerns? Amen.

Day 89

How great is the mercy of the Lord, and his forgiveness for those who turn to him!   —*Ecclus.* 17:29

Often fill your mind with thoughts of the great gentleness and mercy with which God our Savior welcomes souls at death, if they have spent their lives in trusting Him, and striven to serve and love him.   —St. Francis de Sales

Jesus, You spoke often about the danger of offending God so greatly by our sins that we would be worthy only of hell-fire. If we could not be motivated to do good out of love, You wanted us to do good out of fear. Yet you forgave such sinners as Matthew and Mary Magdalene. When we think of our sins, we can have nightmares dreading the punishment of Hell. Instead, inspire us to think of how we might rush to forgive a child who was eager to do good but was ashamed of having failed. Amen.

Day 90

"If you are willing and obedient, you shall eat the good of the land." —Is. 1:19

No one at all can reach eternal life if he be not obedient, for the door was unlocked by the key of obedience, which had been fastened by the disobedience of Adam. I, then, being constrained by My infinite goodness, since I saw that man whom I so much loved, did not return to Me, his End, took the keys of obedience and placed them in the hands of My sweet and amorous Word—the Truth—and He becoming the porter of that door, opened it, and no one can enter except by means of that door and that Porter. When He returned to Me, He left you this sweet key of obedience; for as you know He left His vicar, the Christ, on earth, whom you are all obliged to obey until death, and whoever is outside His obedience is in a state of damnation.

—From a vision granted to St. Catherine of Genoa

Saint Catherine, we may find God's words to you here a little shocking. We don't think that non-Catholics are damned if, in fact, they try to follow the light they see in the areas of faith and morals. Just the same we must continually pray for the reunion of all Christians, so that all may be able to obey God speaking through the true Church. We, who have the full light of truth through the authority of the pope and the bishops when they are united to Him, must be swift to obey that authority. Holy Spirit, help us to be willing to study the teachings of the Vicar of Christ so as to possess the sweet key of obedience needed to pass through the door to eternal life. Amen.

Day 91

The last enemy to be destroyed is death.   —*1 Cor.* 15:26

Eternity always at hand! I look to the far, so far distant shore, the heaven of heavens—a few days more and Eternity—now, then, all resignation . . . rest in Him—the heart in sweet bitterness. Abandon.

What a moment, the greatest, the decisive moment of this earth—the soul passing to eternity—happy eternity for her! O My God! Silence and tears for us who remain in the land of our exile.
                                          —St. Elizabeth Seton

St. Elizabeth Seton, wonderful American widow Saint, we thank you for these words. How they contrast with that fear of death we feel for ourselves and our loved ones! You admit that the death of your daughter caused bitterness, even when there was sweetness because of her innocence. But what a grace for that dying one to have at her bedside a woman of such great faith. Please intercede for us, St. Elizabeth, that we may view death and eternity as you do, so that we may be able to console those who die and witness to faith in Jesus on our own deathbeds. Amen.

Day 92

"Let me die the death of the righteous, and let my end be like his!" —*Num.* 23:10

Yesterday morning, in a meeting that I had with my loving God, I asked Him to detach me from everything, to free me from my body, and having thus broken every bond, to let me go straight to Him, to Him only and forever. —St. Gemma Galgani

St. Gemma, your words help us to know that it is not wrong to pray for death. In our times we have trouble with this. Because of euthanasia, where lives are shortened to avoid pain or sometimes just for convenience or closure, some of us think that if we are pro-life we should never pray for death. When there are close family members or others who are dependent on us, we should certainly pray not for death but for healing. On the other hand, when we believe we have fulfilled the works God wanted us to do on earth and we are lingering in pain, we can pray for death as the gate to union with God in eternity. Guardian Angels, loosen our grip on this world, so that we can come, hands open and outstretched, to greet our Creator and Redeemer. Amen.

Day 93

"I am the living bread which came down from heaven; if any one eats of this bread, he will live forever; and the bread which I shall give for the life of the world is my flesh."   —John 6:51

All souls in hell are there because they did not pray. All the saints in heaven sanctified themselves by prayer.

He who receives Holy Communion most frequently will be freest from sin, and will make farthest progress in Divine Love.

Act as if every day were the last of your life, and each action the last you perform.   —St. Alphonsus Liguori

Lord Jesus, some of us are able to go to Mass and receive You daily but many of us are not. For those of us whose duties or circumstances rule out such a blessing, grant us the grace of spiritual communion by praying, "Lord, I cannot now receive You in Holy Communion, but come spiritually into my heart, now and forever." May we long for these graces so that Your love may fill our hungry hearts. Amen.

Day 94

Since the rosary is a most excellent prayer focused on Jesus and His Life and activities in salvation history, it brings us closer to Our Lord and Our Lady. Doctrinally, Our Lady is our Mother and Jesus is our Eldest Brother, besides being our God.
—"Our Lady's 15 Promises for Praying the Rosary";
cf., Lumen Gentium, chap. VIII—Our Lady, 62

If you say the rosary faithfully until death, I do assure you that, in spite of the gravity of your sins 'you shall receive a never-fading crown of glory. Even if you are on the brink of damnation, even if you have one foot in hell, even if you have sold your soul to the devil as sorcerers do who practice black magic, and even if you are a heretic as obstinate as a devil, sooner or later you will be converted and will amend your life and will save your soul, if—and mark well what I say—if you say the Holy Rosary devoutly every day until death for the purpose of knowing the truth and obtaining contrition and pardon for your sins. —St. Louis de Montfort

Our Lady of the Rosary, not long ago if we had read those words about practicing black magic, we would have thought them to be about people many centuries before! But alas, in the vacuum created today by disbelief in the Christian faith, many have fallen into all kinds of satanic rites or dangerous practices more subtle in their evil origins. Mother Mary, to combat the many errors of this age, we pray that the Rosary may bring us contrition of heart and knowledge of the truth. Amen.

Day 95

So Jesus said to them, "Truly, truly, I say to you, unless you eat the flesh of the Son of man and drink his blood, you have no life in you; he who eats my flesh and drinks my blood has eternal life, and I will raise him up at the last day."   —John 6:53–54

Now there is no distinction made here between soul and body. Christ's blessed Supper is food to us altogether, whatever we are, soul, body, and all. It is the seed of eternal life within us, the food of immortality, to "preserve our body and soul unto everlasting life." The forbidden fruit wrought in Adam unto death; but this is the fruit which makes us live forever. Bread sustains us in this temporal life; the consecrated bread is the means of eternal strength for soul and body. Who could live this visible life without earthly food? And in the same general way the Supper of the Lord is the "means" of our living for ever. We have no reason for thinking we shall live forever unless we eat it, no more than we have reason to think our temporal life will be sustained without meat and drink.   —Bl. John Henry Cardinal Newman

Jesus, institutor of the Sacraments, those of us who are able to go to daily Mass and love to receive You daily in Holy Communion, lament that others who are not infirm and could easily come daily choose instead to go to Church only on the weekend. Perhaps they have never considered the great benefits of daily communion. May their Guardian Angels urge them to find a way to do so. Amen.

Day 96

But Jesus said, "Let the children come to me, and do not hinder them; for to such belongs the kingdom of heaven."

—*Matt.* 19:14

I have always wanted to become a saint. Unfortunately when I have compared myself with the saints, I have always found that there is the same difference between the saints and me as there is between a mountain whose summit is lost in the clouds and a humble grain of sand trodden underfoot by passers-by. Instead of being discouraged, I told myself: God would not make me wish for something impossible and so, in spite of my littleness, I can aim at being a saint. It is impossible for me to grow bigger, so I put up with myself as I am, with all my countless faults. But I will look for some means of going to heaven by a little way which is very short and very straight, a little way that is quite new. What attracts me to the kingdom of Heaven is the call of our Lord, the hope of loving Him as I have so desired and the thought that I shall be able to make Him loved by a great number of souls who will bless Him forever.

—St. Thérèse of Lisieux

Little Thérèse, when you wrote these words you surely didn't know that the whole Catholic world would someday know of your special way of holiness. You write that you had no merits, but we know that accepting every little pin prick of frustration in daily life with a smile is no small merit! Please intercede for us. May we offer up for our own salvation and those around us every difficulty we go through each day. May we also offer up in union with Jesus our humiliating sense of our own unworthiness. Pray us into Heaven! Amen.

Day 97

"Blessed are the pure in heart, for they shall see God."

—*Matt.* 5:8

To bear my exile now, within this world of tears,
The holy tender glance of Christ, my Lord, I need.
That glance, surcharged with love, consoles me through the
*   years;*
His loveliness displays foretaste of heaven indeed.
On me my Jesus smiles, when toward Him I aspire,
The trial of my faith then weighs no more on me.
That love glance of my God, that smile of holy fire,
Oh, this is heaven for me!   —St. Thérèse of Lisieux

St. Thérèse, we read your beautiful words and think how Jesus loved them. Even if we think we cannot write well, we ask our Angels to help us write our own hymn of love. Amen.

Day 98

"Having the eyes of your hearts enlightened, that you may know what is the hope to which he has called you, what are the riches of his glorious inheritance in the saints." —Eph. 1:18

O Eternal Word, Utterance of my God, I long to pass my life listening to You, to become wholly docile, that I may learn all from You. Through all darkness, all privations, all powerlessness, I yearn to keep my eyes ever fixed on You and to dwell beneath Your great light. O my beloved Star, so fascinate me that I can no longer withdraw from Your radiance. —St. Elizabeth of the Trinity

St. Elizabeth of the Trinity, you were a prize-winning pianist, and we find all your words have a musical cadence to them. We imagine that just as you knew the beauty of the darker passages in musical compositions, you were willing to accept that the beauty of Christ mysteriously appears in the soul, even in the midst of pain and weakness, to bring hope. Can you pray for us, not yet so holy, who only want to give up when we feel bad? Amen.

Day 99

"Look at the birds of the air: they neither sow nor reap nor gather into barns, and yet your heavenly Father feeds them. Are you not of more value than they? And which of you by being anxious can add one cubit to his span of life? And why are you anxious about clothing? Consider the lilies of the field, how they grow; they neither toil nor spin; yet I tell you, even Solomon in all his glory was not arrayed like one of these. But if God so clothes the grass of the field, which today is alive and tomorrow is thrown into the oven, will he not much more clothe you, O men of little faith? Therefore do not be anxious, saying, 'What shall we eat?' or 'What shall we drink?' or 'What shall we wear?'"   —Matt. 6:26–31

Pray, hope, and don't worry.   —St. Padre Pio

St. Padre Pio, some Saints wrote long classics on spirituality. Others, like you, left us pieces of advice that, though short, could change our lives totally! How it hurts the Sacred Heart of our Jesus that even His most devout followers don't trust Him but think, instead, that it is better to chew over every future possibility with mingled dread and pathetic hope in human solutions! Pray for us from your heavenly post that we may be liberated from such folly. Amen.

Day 100

*"Now may our Lord Jesus Christ himself, and God our
Father, who loved us and gave us eternal comfort and good hope
through grace, comfort your hearts and establish them in every
good work and word."*   —2 Thess. 2:16–17

*In the moment of temptation think of the Love that awaits
you in heaven: foster the virtue of hope.* —St. Josemaría Escrivá

St. Josemaría Escrivá, founder of the great ecclesial movement Opus Dei, you directed countless men and women in
every role in life. Would you wish us now to review our most
frequent temptations to sin: uncontrolled anger, lust, laziness,
overeating, gossip, drinking too much alcohol? You pinpoint
the attraction—we seek compensation for our feelings of not
having enough love in our lives. We cannot make others love us
as we wish, but if we contemplate the divine love that awaits us
in Heaven we can become willing to bear our present crosses.
Lead us to Eucharistic adoration or simply to the tabernacle to
give Jesus a chance to fill our empty hearts. Amen.

Day 101

So faith, hope, love abide, these three; but the greatest of these is love.   *—1 Cor.* 13:13

I am not sure exactly what Heaven will be like. But I know that when we die and if comes the time for God to judge us, He will not ask, "How many good things have you done in your life?" Rather He will ask, "How much love did you put into what you did?"
                                                       —Bl. Teresa of Calcutta

Blessed Mother Teresa, winner of the Noble Peace Prize for your work with the poorest of the poor, you went from being a missionary school teacher from Albania, unknown to the wider world, to becoming the most famous Catholic sister of the twentieth century. You taught us that we don't need to go all the way to India to serve the poor, because the poor are right among us: on the streets of our rich countries, in the neglected members of our own families, in the tiny persons of the unborn. From Heaven, pray for each of us who read this book that we may put love into everything we do as we prepare for a Heaven of love. Amen.

APPENDIX A

Deathbed Scenes
of Selected Saints

As an end to this chapter on preparing for Heaven we thought you might like to read accounts of the deathbed experiences of some of the Saints. It would be impossible to find all of them, so we are just providing you with a sampling of those we found while researching other topics.

To whet your appetite for the inspiring stories to come, here is an account of what St. Francis of Assisi wrote concerning how the sinner dies:

> The body sickens, death approaches. The relatives and friends come and say, "Prepare thy house!" And the wife and children, his nearest ones and his friends, act as if they wept. And the sick one looks around then sees them weep and is moved by a false emotion and thinks to himself, "Yes, I will give over myself with soul and body and all that I have into your faithful hands!" Truly the man is damned, who gives his soul, his body and all that he has, into such hands and depends upon them! The priest says to him, "Dost thou wish to do penance for all thy transgressions?" The sick man answers, "Yes." And the priest asks, "Wilt thou give reparation to all whom thou hast defrauded and betrayed, as afar

as thou canst?" He answers, "No." And the priest says, "Why not?" He answers, "Because I have given all to my family and to my friends." And thereby he misses his goal.[1]

An Account of Mary's Death as Told by St. Alphonsus Liguori

She then decently composed herself on her poor little bed, where she laid herself to await death, and with it the meeting with the Divine Spouse, who shortly was to come and take her with Him to the kingdom of the blessed. Behold, she already feels in her heart a great joy, the forerunner of the coming of the Bridegroom, which inundates her with an unaccustomed and novel sweetness . . . And she, the most loving Mother, compassionated all, and consoled each one (the Apostles); to some promising her patronage, blessing others with particular affection, and encouraging others to the work of the conversion of the world; especially she called Saint Peter to her, and as head of the Church and Vicar of her Son, recommended to him in a particular manner the propagation of the Faith, promising him at the same time her especial protection in heaven.

But more particularly did she call Saint John to her, who more than any other was grieved at this moment when he had to part with his holy Mother; and the most gracious Lady, remembering the affection and attention with which this holy disciple had served her during all the years she had remained on earth since the death of her Son,

---

said: "My own John, I thank thee for all the assistance thou hast afforded me; my son, be assured of it, I shall not be ungrateful. If I now leave thee, I go to pray for thee. Remain in peace in this life until we meet again in heaven, where I await thee. Never forget me. In all thy wants call me to thy aid; for I will never forget thee, my beloved son. Son, I bless thee. I leave thee my blessing. Remain in peace. Farewell!"

Mary, then, has left this world; she is now in heaven. Thence does this compassionate Mother look down upon us who are still in this valley of tears. She pities us, and, if we wish it, promises to help us. Let us always beseech her, by the merits of her blessed death, to obtain us a happy death; and should such be the good pleasure of God, let us beg her to obtain us the grace to die on a Saturday, which is a day dedicated in her honor, or on a day of a novena, or within the octave of one of her feasts.[2]

St. Perpetua's Dream of Heaven, as Told to Her Brother

I beheld a ladder of bronze, marvelously great, reaching up to heaven; and it was narrow, so that not more than one might go up at one time. And in the sides of the ladder were planted all manner of things of iron. There were swords there, spears, hooks, and knives; so that if any that went up took not good heed or looked not upward, he would be torn and his flesh cling to the iron. And there was right at the ladder's foot a serpent lying, marvelously

2   "Saint Alphonsus de Liguori—Of the Assumption of Mary," http://saints.sqpn.com/sta09003.htm.

great, which lay in wait for those that would go up, and frightened them that they might not go up. Now Saturus went up first (who afterwards had of his own free will given up himself for our sakes, because it was he who had edified us; and when we were taken he had not been there). And he came to the ladder's head; and he turned and said: "Perpetua, I await you; but see that serpent bite you not."

And I said: it shall not hurt me, in the name of Jesus Christ. And from beneath the ladder, as though it feared me, it softly put forth its head; and as though I trod on the first step I trod on its head. And I went up, and I saw a very great space of garden, and in the midst a man sitting, white-headed, in shepherd's clothing, tall milking his sheep; and standing around in white were many thousands. And he raised his head and beheld me and said to me: Welcome, child. And he cried to me, and from the curd he had from the milk he gave me as it were a morsel; and I took it with joined hands and ate it up; and all that stood around said, Amen. And at the sound of that word I awoke, yet eating I know not what of sweet.[3]

The Death of St. Cyril

When the time came for him to set out from the world to the peace of his heavenly homeland, he prayed to God with his hands outstretched and his eyes filled with tears: "O Lord, my God, you have created the choirs of angels and spiritual powers; you have stretched forth the heavens and established the earth, creating all that exists from nothing.

---

3   "St. Perpetua: The Passion of Saints Perpetua and Felicity," Medieval Sourcebook, http://www.fordham.edu/halsall/source/perpetua.html.

Once he had exchanged the gift of peace with everyone," he said: "Blessed be God who did not hand us over to our invisible enemy, but freed us from his snare and delivered us from perdition." He then fell asleep in the Lord.[4]

The Death of St. Scholastica

Three days later, Benedict was in his cell. Looking up to the sky, he saw his sister's soul leave her body in the form of a dove, and fly up to the secret places of heaven.[5]

The following is a vision reported from the deathbed of Blessed Angela of Foligno:[6]

Behold, the moment has arrived in which my God fulfills his promise to me. Christ, his Son, has now presented me to the Father. You know how when Christ was in the boat, there were great storms? Truly, it is sometimes like that with the soul. He permits storms to assail it, and he seems to sleep. In truth, God at times allows a person to be completely broken and downtrodden before he puts an end to the storm.

Then she was told by Jesus: "O my spouse, my beautiful one, I love you with great affection. I do not want you to come to me burdened with these pains and sorrows, but jubilant and filled with ineffable joy. For it is only fitting for a king to wed his long-loved bride, clothed in royal garment. I do not entrust to either the angels or any other

---

4   *Liturgy of the Hours,* "Office of Readings, February 14."
5   *Liturgy of the Hours,* "Office of Readings February 10."
6   Romana Guarnieri, *Angela of Foligno: Complete Works,* trans. Paul Lachance (New York: Paulist Press, 1993), 313.

saints the task of bringing you to me. I will come for you in person and I will take you with me."

The following is more from the writings of witnesses of Blessed Angela's death:[7]

Christ rejoicing and with joy unspeakable, even as it is seemly that the King should lead home the bride whom He hath loved so long, and clothed with the royal robe.

And he showed me the robe, even as the bridegroom showeth it unto the bride whom he hath loved a long time. It was neither of purple nor of scarlet, nor of sendal, nor of samite, but it was a certain marvelous light which clothed the soul. And then He showed unto me the Bridegroom, the Eternal Word, so that now I do understand what thing the Word is and what it doth mean that is to say, this Word which for my sake was made Flesh.

And the Word entered into me and touched me throughout and embraced me, saying, "Come, My love, My bride, beloved of Me with true delight come, for all the saints do await thee with exceeding great joy. And He said again unto me, I will not commit thee in charge unto the blessed angels or other saints that they should lead thee unto Me, but I will come personally and fetch thee and will raise thee unto Myself, for thou hast made thyself meet for Me and pleasing unto My Majesty."

Now when she was nigh unto the time of her passing away (being the day before it), she did often repeat, "Father, into Thy Hands I do commend my soul and my spirit." Once, after repeating these words, she said unto us

7   Mary G. Steegmann, trans., *The Book Of Divine Consolation of the Blessed Angela of Foligno* (New York: Duffield, 1909), 262–63.

who were present, "Now hath an answer unto those words been given unto me, and it is this: It is impossible that in death thou shouldst lose that which hath been impressed upon thine heart in life."

The following is an account of the death of St. Teresa of Avila by an eyewitness, Sr. Maria of St. Francis:[8]

On the morning of the feast of St. Francis, (St. Teresa) turned on her side toward the nuns, a crucifix in her hand, her expression more beautiful, more glowing, than I had ever seen it during her life. I do not know how her wrinkles disappeared, since the Holy Mother, in view of her great age and her continual suffering had very deep ones. She remained in this position in prayer full of deep peace and great repose. Occasionally she gave some outward sign of surprise or amazement. But everything proceeded in great repose. It seemed as if she were hearing a voice that she answered. Her facial expression was so wondrously changed that it looked like a celestial body to us. Thus immersed in prayer, happy and smiling, she went out of this world into eternal life.

The Death of St. Elizabeth Seton

As I placed the ciborium upon the little table, she (Elizabeth) burst into tears and sobbing aloud covered her face with her two hands. I thought first that it was some fear of sin, and approaching her, I asked. "Have you any pain? Do

---

8   Waltraut Stein, trans., *Love for Love: Life and Works of St. Teresa of Jesus* (Washington, DC: ICS Publications, 1992), 65.

you wish to confess?" "No, no, only give him to me," as she said with an ardor, a kind of exclamation and her whose pale face was so inflamed that I was much affected and repeating, "Peace, dear Mother, receive with great peace your God of peace." She whispered, "One Communion more and then Eternity."[9]

At the Deathbed of St. Alphonsus Liguori

Each night I pray to God to take me out of this wretched world, but every dawn finds me still here, writhing in physical and mental torture with even my spirit in near despair. Mine is a living death, I can call it nothing else. I am hanging onto my sanity by a mere thread. Oh, compassionate Jesus, be merciful to me a sinner. Mary, Mother of the Redeemer and my mother, let me not be lost for all eternity. Saint Joseph, patron of a happy death, at least let me die at peace with myself and my brethren. Grant that I may love thee always, sweet Lord, and then, do with me whatever thou wilt. Amen, so do I hope, so may it be.[10]

The Death of Brother Andre

One doesn't think about death enough. Sickness is a good thing because it helps us reflect on our past life and make

9   Ellin M. Kelly and Annabelle Melville, *Selected Writings of Elizabeth Ann Seton* (New York: Paulist Press, 1987), 255ff.

10 Joseph Oppitz, *Autumn Memoirs of St. Alphonsus Liguori* (Liguori, MO: Liguori Publications, 1986), 74–5.

reparations through penitence and through suffering (After a violent attack of pain he said), The Great Almighty is coming! Heaven is so beautiful that it is worth all the trouble with which one prepares for it. How beautiful God is, since the soul, which is but a ray of His beauty, is so lovely.[11]

The following is an account by Celine, sister of St. Thérèse, about her father, Ven. Louis Martin:[12]

[After an illness we now think was Alzheimer's:] I will always remember his beautiful face when, in the evening, as night fell in the deep woods, we stopped to hear a nightingale: he listened . . . with what expression in his gaze! It was like an ecstasy, some inexpressible part of heaven was reflected in his features. Then after a good moment of silence, we were still listening, and I saw tears streaming down his dear cheeks.

The Last Words of Pope John XXIII

We are about to enter the tabernacle of the Lord. "I know in whom I have believed. I have been able to follow my own death step by step and now I am going gently to my end."[13]

When Mother Teresa of Calcutta knew she was near to death, she said, "God doesn't make mistakes."

---

11 C. Bernard Ruffin, *The Life of Brother Andre the Miracle Worker of St. Joseph* (Huntington, IN: Our Sunday Visitor, 1988), 192.

12 Stephane-Joseph Piat, *Celine: Sister Genevieve of the Holy Face* (San Francisco: Ignatius Press, 1997), 58.

13 Paul Johnson, *Pope John XXIII* (Boston: Little Brown, 1974), 232.

APPENDIX B
Difficult Questions about the Afterlife

Will Everyone Eventually Be in Heaven?

Without a doubt, it is a terrible exercise to contemplate the fate of the damned. To even try to imagine the unending wretchedness in Hell of those who die in a state of mortal sin, who willingly and freely reject everlasting life with God in Heaven and forever separate themselves from communion with Him, fills the human imagination with a sense of unspeakable dread, horror, and sorrow. Eternal damnation is not a subject that should be taken lightly.

Perhaps that is one reason why many people reject the traditional understanding that the damned will suffer eternal punishment in Hell in favor of the belief that all people (some say even Satan and the demons) eventually will be redeemed and admitted to Heaven. This belief in the ultimate universal salvation of all humankind through Jesus Christ (known variably as the doctrine of universalism, *apocatastasis*, or universal reconciliation) has its origins among several theologians and schools of thought in the early centuries of Christianity. Although condemned by St. Augustine, the Fifth Ecumenical Council, Pope

Vigilius, Pope St. Gregory the Great and others, the notion survived over the centuries in various forms in certain pockets of Christianity while usually being considered a heresy by the orthodox majority.

It is apparent that over the centuries many Christians have accepted one form of this belief or another and not in insignificant numbers, even within some contemporary Catholic circles. However, is this belief compatible with the teachings of the Church?

The Church infallibly teaches as a matter of revealed dogma that Hell exists, that it is an eternal state, and that it is possible for humans to go there. All Catholics are required to give the assent of Divine Faith to this teaching: "To die in mortal sin without repenting and accepting God's merciful love means remaining separated from him forever by our own free choice. This state of definitive self-exclusion from communion with God . . . is called 'hell.'"[1] In addition, "The teaching of the Church affirms the existence of hell and its eternity. Immediately after death the souls of those who die in a state of mortal sin descend into hell, where they suffer the punishments of hell, 'eternal fire.' The chief punishment of hell is eternal separation from God, in whom alone man can possess the life and happiness for which he was created and for which he longs."[2] Any person who dies in this final condition of freely chosen impenitence experiences a fixation of the will in opposition to God, as well as an immutably fixed state of being—the state of eternal damnation. But would any soul actually make such a choice, knowing the consequences?

As difficult as it may be to comprehend, it is possible. An individual who has spent his life in rebellion against God in the

---

1   *CCC*, 1033, 292.
2   *CCC*, 1035, 292.

pursuit of sinful self-interest, and who reaches the end of his life in the condition of mortal sin, may find that he has been so formed in disobedience that his will is hardened against God even at this crucial moment, so much so that he obstinately and tragically continues to refuse to repent to the very end. Nevertheless, some would ask, would a loving God condemn even such a person as this to an eternity in Hell? Universalists, and those who sympathize with them, would say that the answer is no, that God who is perfect love and mercy would never condemn any soul to eternal damnation. To do so, they argue, would be contrary to His very nature and would undermine the sufficiency of Christ's sacrifice for the redemption of the entire world. However, while it is true that perfect love and mercy are attributes of God, one must not forget that perfect justice also is an attribute of God. They do not cancel each other out or contradict each other, but they are each seamlessly united and fulfilled in the Divine Will.

God has endowed every person with freedom of will that enables him, with the help of His grace, to choose that which is good and holy, and leads to eternal life with Him. By the same token, each person, in his freedom, is able to misuse that freedom by rejecting that which is good and holy, and consequently follow a path that leads to eternal death and separation from God. There are, of course, conditions and circumstances that can possibly lessen the culpability of such an abuse of freedom (e.g., certain psychological disorders or mental disabilities), but generally speaking, people are free to make moral choices that have particular consequences. This means that they are free to turn from God, His love, and His mercy and go their own way.

God's perfect justice demands that human moral choices freely made be honored, even if that choice entails the embrace of mortal sin and an eternal rejection of God. Christ's Passion is certainly sufficient to redeem everyone from the consequences of sin, but the mercy of God thus offered is not forced. No one is compelled to friendship with God. The human will must assent to the reception of His love and mercy. It is possible then that there are those who willfully choose to exclude themselves from God's friendship and condemn themselves to eternal separation from Him in Hell. To those who may make that terrible choice, God will finally say, "Thy will be done." For God to do otherwise would be to strip the person of his freedom of will, an essential aspect of what it means to be human.

Having said this, however, we must be careful to point out that the Church has never made a pronouncement that any particular human being is in Hell. Only God is privy to such knowledge. Rather, the Church admonishes all the faithful to hope for, pray for, and work for the salvation of all people. As the *Catechism* states, "The Church prays that no one should be lost: 'Lord, let me never be parted from you.' If it is true that no one can save himself, it is also true that God 'desires all men to be saved' (*1 Tim.* 2:4), and that for him 'all things are possible' (*Matt.* 19:26)."[3]

And further, "We can therefore hope in the glory of heaven promised by God to those who love him and do his will. In every circumstance, each one of us should hope, with the grace of God, to persevere 'to the end' and to obtain the joy of heaven, as God's eternal reward for the good works accomplished with the grace of Christ. In hope, the Church prays for "all men to be saved."[4] Some theologians, and even canonized Saints, have augmented this hope with the belief that prior to the moment of death, God comes to even the most consistently impenitent and hardened of sinners to offer them a final opportunity to

---

3   *CCC*, 1058, 298.
4   *CCC*, 1821, 500.

repent and receive His forgiveness. A well-known example of this final act of Divine grace is recounted by St. Faustina, the Apostle of Divine Mercy, in *Diary*:

> Then the mercy of God begins to exert itself, and, without any cooperation from the soul, God grants it final grace. If this too is spurned, God will leave the soul in this self-chosen disposition for eternity. This grace emerges from the merciful Heart of Jesus and gives the soul a special light by means of which the soul begins to understand God's effort; but conversion depends on its own will. The soul knows that this, for her, is final grace and, should it show even a flicker of good will, the mercy of God will accomplish the rest.[5]

Even as we hold this hope in our hearts for ourselves and for others, one should be careful not to take the grace of God for granted. We must be cautious never to rely on a presumed opportunity for a last minute conversion in order to be reconciled with God. Even though the disclosure of final Divine Mercy to St. Faustina, as detailed in *Diary of Saint Maria Faustina Kowalska*, is a beautiful and hope-filled vision of God's benevolence, it is nevertheless based on a private revelation and does not have the status of dogma in the Church. None of the faithful is required to give to it the assent of Divine Faith, as they must do for doctrines that have been publicly defined by the infallible teaching authority of the Church. Instead, they are only encouraged to respect it using the virtue of prudence and may give to it the assent of human faith. Consequently, we would do well

---

5 *Diary of Saint Maria Faustina Kowalska: Divine Mercy in my Soul* (3rd ed.), Marian Press: 2003, 1486.

always to live a circumspect life and habitually pray and labor not only for the salvation of others but for our own determined perseverance in grace so that we may depart this life in the sure friendship and love of God and at the end be counted among those who will behold His face in glory everlasting.

How Can We Be Happy in Heaven if Our Loved Ones Don't Get There?

Another concern people commonly voice has to do with the possibility of souls being condemned to Hell for all eternity. Some may even fear that their loved ones might not be with them in Heaven. "How can one be happy in Heaven," it is said, "if my loved ones are not there with me to enjoy it?"

That is a very good question. Even though the Church does not teach that most people go to Hell, from a limited human perspective, it would seem that the perfect happiness of Heaven would be unachievable if someone we dearly loved was eternally absent from its joys, even more so if we knew that such an individual was suffering the eternal torments of the damned. I can readily understand how a loving mother, for example, might believe herself to be inconsolable in Heaven if she knew that one of her children was in Hell. How can such an objection be addressed?

In seeking to answer this question, various theologians have resorted to solutions that are in conflict with the sacred scriptures and the magisterial teachings of the Church. Some have espoused the theory of universalism; others have proposed that the redeemed souls in Heaven simply will forget all about their earthly relations and not be troubled by memories of past associations. This is also not supported by either Scripture or tradition (e.g., *Luke* 16:27–28), however. So how does one deal with this painful question?

The first point that must be asserted when contemplating this problem is an affirmation that the redeemed will most certainly be happy in Heaven, regardless of whether or not any particular loved one is absent from that state of bliss. St. John tells us that in Heaven all sadness resulting from the changes and chances of life will be removed. Concerning the redeemed, he remarks that "the Lamb in the midst of the throne will be their shepherd, and he will guide them to springs of living water; and God will wipe away every tear from their eyes" (*Rev.* 7:17). Thus it is of a surety that all sadness, even that which one might reasonably expect to experience over the loss of an absent loved one, will be unknown in Heaven. In fact, the redeemed souls in Heaven will experience only complete joy, no matter the circumstances of family or friends.

Why? The experience of perfect joy, resulting in the absence of all sadness, is grounded in the Beatific Vision. The *Catechism* teaches that "the Beatific Vision, in which God opens himself in an inexhaustible way to the elect, will be the ever-flowing well-spring of happiness, peace, and mutual communion."[6] The souls in Heaven will be so united with God that they will be completely and perfectly fulfilled. St. Thomas Aquinas writes in the *Summa Contra Gentiles* that the redeemed will "enjoy the same happiness wherewith God is happy, seeing Him in the way in which He sees Himself."[7] Because of this, they will be unaffected by any lesser, contrary thing or experience,

---

6 *CCC*, 1045, 295.
7 *Of God and His Creatures: An Annotated Translation of the* Summa Contra Gentiles *of Saint Thomas Aquinas*, Joseph Rickaby, S.J., London: Burns and Oates, 1905, 225.

including sadness. Their happiness will be immutable, absolute, and unassailable.

Moreover, if any of their loved ones are in Hell, the redeemed in Heaven will understand and accept that fact with unspoiled serenity and perfect charity. Flowing from their union with God, they will see lost souls as God sees each and every one of them. The Beatific Vision will bestow such deep insight and profound understanding that all will be able to comprehend fully and affirm completely the justice of God with regard to the damned. This justice confirms the freedom of will that human beings possess and the ability of each in that same freedom to reject God and to embrace self-exclusion from Heaven. Although God's love for the damned is far greater than human love can comprehend, His respect for the freedom of each individual is absolute. The decision, then, to turn one's face away from God, a decision exercised in free will, is a personal choice that God will not violate.

Finally, it must be considered that in some sense, the ability of individuals to self-exclude from Heaven is, in itself, a mercy given by God. If a person so despised God that he or she would loathe to be in the holy presence of the Almighty, then to allow them to go their own way would in actuality be a loving act. Otherwise to force anyone proverbially to bend the knee in the company of God would be torturous, an affront to the dignity of human freedom. In the end, for God to say to the damned, "Thy will be done," is the granting of their own desire to separate themselves from the Divine Presence, a much more loving act than for God to force an eternal obeisance.

And so, as we contemplate the hope of our future repose in the heavenly presence of God, we should do so in the sure and certain knowledge that, regardless of who else may be there, we will experience a supreme and unending joy centered in God Himself.

APPENDIX C
Purgatory

In the Sacred Scriptures we read, "it is a holy and pious thought. Therefore he made atonement for the dead, that they might be delivered from their sin" (*2 Mach.* 12:45). If the dead are in Hell, they cannot benefit from our prayers. If they are in Heaven, they do not need our prayers. Therefore there must be a state where the dead can be helped by the prayers of the living faithful. The Church calls this state Purgatory. So what is Purgatory?

Purgatory, according to the *Catechism*, is that state wherein "all who die in God's grace and friendship, but still imperfectly purified, are indeed assured of their eternal salvation; but after death they undergo purification, so as to achieve the holiness necessary to enter the joy of heaven."[1] This purification, according to Church tradition, will involve "a cleansing fire."[2]

I would suspect that most all of us will depart this life with some unfinished business, spiritually speaking. Even if we die in the state of grace in friendship with God, we likely will still have some imperfections that we were unable to overcome during our lifetime. These could include improper attachments to

---

1   *CCC,* 1030, 291.
2   *CCC,* 1031, 291.

certain venial sins or even lesser goods; unhealthy habits and inclinations toward which we were disposed; undue attitudes and proclivities of body, mind, and spirit that were not perfectly oriented toward the glory of God, our sanctification and that of others, and so forth. All these sorts of faults, and more, will require purification before our sanctification is complete and we are perfected in holiness, made ready to stand in the nearer presence of God in Heaven.

Moreover, even though we die in the state of grace, and through the sacrifice of Christ have been forgiven the eternal punishment in Hell that our sins rightly deserved, there may still remain the temporal punishment due our sins. What is temporal punishment? The word "temporal" means "time." Put very simply, temporal punishment is the suffering in this life "in time" that we may experience due to the consequences that flow from our sins.

An imperfect, though perhaps helpful, illustration of temporal punishment might be the following. Imagine a child playing in her mother's flower garden. The beautiful flowers are filled with honeybees from a nearby hive gathering nectar. The mother has told the child repeatedly not to bother the bees, not to touch them, or try to pick them up, because they could sting and hurt her. But the child is headstrong and determined and thinks she knows better than her mother about honeybees. So she decides to pick up a bee that is resting on a flower and the bee stings her. The child cries out in pain and runs to her mother with tears streaming down her face. Of course, the mother removes the stinger, forgives the child's disobedience and consoles her, but that doesn't take away the hurt, swelling, and itching resulting from the sting. The child still has to "pay the piper," so to speak, and suffer the pain that is a consequence of her disobedience. Temporal punishment for sin is similar to this.

In this life, we may not pay completely the satisfaction due our sins because we do not fully experience the sanctifying purification that necessarily flows from the deserved temporal punishment. In that case, we must then do so in Purgatory after we die.

There are, however, opportunities in this life that can be accessed by the faithful before we die in order to lessen the degree of satisfaction that will be required of us because of the temporal punishment due our sins. The Church teaches us that "the forgiveness of sin and restoration of communion with God entail the remission of the eternal punishment of sin, but temporal punishment of sin remains. While patiently bearing sufferings and trials of all kinds and, when the day comes, serenely facing death, the Christian must strive to accept this temporal punishment of sin as a grace. He should strive by works of mercy and charity, as well as by prayer and the various practices of penance, to put off completely the 'old man' and to put on the 'new man.'"[3] Through our penitential efforts and good works, our prayers, our charity, and our sufferings patiently endured that are offered up to God and joined to the sacrifice of the cross of Christ, we are enabled by His grace to undergo a conversion of charity and to satisfy in this earthly life—at least in part—the temporal punishment that we would otherwise fulfill in Purgatory in the process of our sanctification. However, there is even more than this.

By means of the authority that Christ gave His Church (to St. Peter, the Apostles, and their successors) in the "power of the keys," the power to "lose and bind," and the power to "forgive and retain sins" (*Matt.* 16:19; 18:18; *John* 20:23), the

---

3   *CCC*, 1473, 411.

Church has the ability to confer the satisfactions from the treasury of the merits of Christ and His Saints upon the faithful for their sanctification. The Church does this by means of granting indulgences that are declarations of the lessening of all or part (plenary indulgences or partial indulgences) of the temporal punishments due an individual's sin. Indulgences are granted after the person seeking them performs particular prescribed acts of penance, prayer, devotion, good works, charity, and the like to which the promised indulgence has been attached. The *Catechism* says that an indulgence is "a remission before God of the temporal punishment due to sins whose guilt has already been forgiven," which the Church, "as the minister of redemption, dispenses and applies with authority the treasury of the satisfactions of Christ and the saints."[4]

The *Catechism* adds that the Church prescribes indulgences not only to help Christians by remitting the temporal punishment from their sins, but "also to spur them to works of devotion, penance, and charity."[5]

Indulgences can be obtained not only for a living person's particular benefit, but also for the benefit of the Holy Souls in Purgatory. Thus our devotional life, and our charitable good works, can benefit not only ourselves but our deceased loved ones as well. The 2006 *Manual of Indulgences*, published by the United States Conference of Catholic Bishops, lists numerous indulgences that are available for the faithful to obtain and clearly describes the norms and grants that are available.

Far from being a fearful or onerous topic, the doctrine of Purgatory as taught by the Catholic Church gives comfort, hope, and peace to all who embrace and implement it in their

---

4   *CCC*, 1471, 411.
5   *CCC*, 1478, 413.

lives. And perhaps, if we endeavor by God's grace to amend our spiritual defects and imperfections, and make use of the means of grace that God makes available to us in this life for our sanctification and the satisfaction of our sins, we may avoid Purgatory altogether. If so, at our last breath, we will be ushered into His very presence. May God, in His mercy, grant this to all those who seek it.

APPENDIX D
Traditional Prayers of the Church

Prayer for the Holy Souls in Purgatory

O Lord, who art ever merciful and bounteous with Thy gifts, look down upon the suffering souls in Purgatory. Remember not their offenses and negligences, but be mindful of Thy loving mercy, which is from all eternity. Cleanse them of their sins and fulfill their ardent desires that they may be made worthy to behold Thee face to face in Thy glory. May they soon be united with Thee and hear those blessed words which will call them to their heavenly home: "Come, blessed of My Father, take possession of the Kingdom prepared for you from the foundation of the world." Amen.

A Prayer to the Lord Jesus (Blessed John Henry Newman)

My Lord and Savior, in your arms I am safe; keep me and I have nothing to fear; give me up and I have nothing to hope for. I pray you not to make me rich, I pray you not to make me very

179

poor; but I leave it all to you, because you know and I do not. If you bring pain or sorrow on me, give me grace to bear it well. If you give me health and strength and success in this world, keep me ever on my guard lest these great gifts carry me away from you. Give me ever to aim at setting forth your glory to live to and for you; to set a good example to all around me; give me to die just at that time and in that way which is most for your glory, and best for my salvation. Amen

A Prayer for Holy Rest
(Blessed John Henry Newman)

May He support us all the day long, till the shadows lengthen, and the evening comes, and the busy world is hushed, and the fever of life is over, and our work is done! Then in His mercy may He give us a safe lodging, and a holy rest, and peace at the last. Amen.

Prayer for a Happy Death

O God, great and omnipotent judge of the living and the dead, we are to appear before You after this short life to render an account of our works. Give us the grace to prepare for our last hour by a devout and holy life, and protect us against a sudden and unprovided death. Let us remember our frailty and mortality, that we may always live in the ways of Your commandments. Teach us to "watch and pray," that when Your summons comes for our departure from this world, we may go forth to meet You, experience a merciful judgment, and rejoice in everlasting happiness. We ask this through Christ our Lord. Amen.

For the Protection of the Holy Family

Grant unto us, Lord Jesus, ever to follow the example of Thy holy Family, that in the hour of our death Thy glorious Virgin Mother together with blessed Joseph may come to meet us and we may be worthily received by Thee into everlasting dwellings: Who livest and reignest world without end. Amen.

To Our Lord for a Happy Death

Lord Jesus Christ, who willest that no man should perish, and to whom petition is never made without the hope of mercy, for Thou saidst with Thine own holy and blessed lips: "All things whatsoever ye shall ask in My name, shall be done unto you"; I beg of Thee, O Lord, for Thy holy Name's sake, to grant me at the hour of my death full consciousness and the power of speech, sincere contrition for my sins, true faith, firm hope and perfect charity, that I may be able to say unto Thee with a clean heart: Thou has redeemed me, O God of truth, who art blessed forever and ever. Amen.

A Prayer When Death is Near

Into Thy hands, Lord, I commend my spirit. Oh, Lord Jesus Christ, receive my spirit.

A Prayer at the Moment of Death

Holy Mary, pray for me. Holy Mary, Mother of grace, Mother of mercy, do thou defend me from the enemy, and receive me at the hour of death.

APPENDIX E
An Examination of Conscience

First Commandment:
I Am the Lord Thy God; Thou Shalt
Not Have Strange Gods before Me

Sins contrary to the
First Commandment are the following:

Neglect of prayer; ingratitude toward God; spiritual sloth; hatred of God or of the Catholic Church; tempting God (explicitly or implicitly, e.g. by exposing one's self to danger of soul, life, or health without grave cause); not behaving reverently when in church (e.g., not genuflecting to the Blessed Sacrament when entering or leaving the church, etc.); excessive attraction to things/creatures (e.g. over-affection to animals, sports fanaticism, having movie star/music/TV idols, love for money, pleasure, or power); idolatry (worshiping false gods such as giving honor to a creature in place of God (e.g. Satan, science,

---

This examination of conscience is in the public domain and can be found at http://www.sensustraditionis.org/ExaminationConscience Long.pdf.

ancestors, country); superstition (ascribing powers to a created thing which it does not have); hypnotism (without sufficient cause); divination (communication with Satan, demons, the dead, or other false practices in order to discover the unknown, consulting horoscopes, astrology, palm reading, fortune telling); attaching undue importance to dreams, omens or lots; all practices of magic or sorcery (e.g. witchcraft, voodoo); wearing charms; playing with Ouija boards or rotating tables; spiritism (talking with the spirits); sacrilege (profaning or treating unworthily the Sacraments, especially the Holy Eucharist, and other liturgical actions, as well as religious persons, blessed things such as sacred vessels or statues, or places consecrated to God); sacrilege by receiving a sacrament, especially the Holy Eucharist, in the state of mortal sin; simony (buying or selling of spiritual things); profane or superstitious use of blessed objects (sometimes done in order to remain in sin); practical materialism (one believes he needs and desires only material things); atheistic humanism (falsely considers man to be an end in himself, and the sole maker with supreme control of his own history); atheism in general (rejects, denies or doubts the existence of God, either in theory or practice, i.e. ignoring Him in the daily living of our lives); agnosticism (postulates the existence of a transcendent being which is incapable of revealing itself, and about which nothing can be said or makes no judgment about God's existence declaring it impossible to prove or even to affirm or deny).

Sins against Faith:

Willful doubt of any article of faith; deliberate ignorance of the truths of faith which ought to be known; neglect of instructing oneself in the faith according to one's state in life; rash credulity (e.g. giving credence to private revelation too easily or believing in a private revelations which has been condemned by the lawful Church authorities); apostasy; heresy; indifferentism (to believe that one religion is as good as another, and that all religions are equally true and pleasing to God, or that one is free to accept or reject any or all religions); reading or circulating books or writings against the Catholic belief or practice in such wise as to jeopardize one's faith; to remain silent when asked about one's faith; engaging is schismatic or heretical worship; joining or supporting Masonic groups or other forbidden societies.

Sins against Hope:

Despair of God's mercy (to give up all hope of salvation, and the means necessary to be saved) or want of confidence in the power of His Grace to support us in trouble or temptation; no desire to possess eternal happiness in heaven or after this earthly life; presumption (to hope for salvation without help from God or to assume God's forgiveness without conversion, or to hope to obtain heavenly glory without merit); presuming on God's mercy or on the supposed efficacy of certain pious practices, in order to continue in sin; refusing any dependence on God.

Sins against Charity:

Not making an act of charity at regular intervals during life especially during times of necessity; egoism (one cares only about himself, praises himself, selfish, enjoys receiving praise) willfully rebellious thoughts against God; boasting of sin; violating God's law, or omitting good works through human respect.

Second Commandment:
Thou Shalt Not Take the Name
of the Lord Thy God in Vain

Sins contrary to the Second Commandment:

Dishonoring of God by profane or disrespectful use of the name of God, or of the Holy name of Jesus Christ, the name of the Blessed Virgin Mary and all the saints; blasphemy (speech or gestures that have contempt for or insult to God, Jesus Christ, the Catholic Church, the Blessed Virgin Mary or the saints); perjury (to promise something under oath with no intention of keeping it, or breaking a promise made under oath); taking false or unnecessary oaths (to call on God to be witness to a lie); breaking vows or promises to God; talking during Mass and in a Church without sufficient reason or to the distraction of others.

Third Commandment: Remember That
Thou Shalt Keep Holy the Lord's Day

Sins contrary to the Third Commandment:

Omission of prayer and divine worship, all unnecessary servile work, and whatever hinders the keeping of the Lord's Day holy; engaging in unnecessary commerce, i.e. buying and selling on Sundays and Holy Days of Obligation.

Fourth Commandment: Honor Thy Father and Thy Mother

Sins contrary to the Fourth Commandment:

For Parents: Hating their children; cursing them; giving scandal to them by cursing, drinking, etc.; allowing them to grow up in ignorance, idleness or sin; showing habitual partiality without cause; deferring a child's baptism; neglecting to watch over their bodily health, their religious instruction, the company they keep, the books they read, etc.; failing to correct them when needful; being harsh or cruel in correction; sending children to Protestant and other dangerous schools; neglect of directing them to attend Holy Mass on Sundays and Holy Days and to frequent reception of the Sacraments.

For Children: All manner of anger or hatred against parents and other lawful superiors; provoking them to anger; grieving them; insulting them; neglecting them in their necessity; contempt or disobedience to their lawful commands.

Husbands and wives: Ill-usage (i.e. using them without consideration for their own welfare and without regard to charity); putting obstacles to the fulfillment of religious duties; want of gentleness and consideration in regard to each other's faults; unreasonable jealousy; neglect of household duties; sulkiness; injurious words; neglect of attempting to secure means of supporting the family due to laziness or timidity.

For Employers: not allowing one's employees reasonable time for religious duties and instruction; giving bad example to them or allowing others to do so; withholding their lawful wages; not caring for them in sickness; dismissing them arbitrarily and without cause; imposing unreasonable policies.

For Employees: disrespect to employers; want of obedience in matters wherein one has bound oneself to obey (e.g. by fulfilling a contract); waste of time; neglect of work; waste of employer's property by dishonesty, carelessness or neglect; violating company policies without sufficient reason.

For Professionals and civil servants: culpable lack of the knowledge relating to duties of office or profession; neglect in discharging those duties; injustice or partiality; exorbitant fees (this sin may also be included under the Seventh Commandment).

For Teachers: neglecting the progress of those confided to their care; unjust, indiscreet or excessive punishment; partiality; bad example; loose or false maxims (i.e. teaching them things which are untrue as being true).

For Students: disrespect; disobedience; stubbornness; idleness; waste of time; giving in to idle distractions (e.g. partying and undue recreating).

For All: contempt for the laws of State and country as well as of the Church; disobedience to lawful authority; breaking of civil laws.

Fifth Commandment: Thou Shalt Not Kill

Sins against the Fifth commandment include:

Murder; performing an abortion; having an abortion, aiding in someone procuring an abortion (the penitent should know that having, causing or aiding in an abortion causing one to be excommunicated); euthanasia; withholding ordinary means to a dying or terminally ill patient; suicide; attempts of suicide, serious thoughts about committing suicide; fighting; quarreling anger; hatred; desires of revenge; human torture; gluttony (excessive eating or drinking); drunkenness; abuse of alcohol, medicine or drugs; endangering other people's lives (e.g. by drinking and driving, by driving too fast, etc.); risking one's own life or limb without a sufficient reason (e.g. daredevil stunts, Russian roulette, etc.); carelessness in leaving about poisons, dangerous drugs, weapons, etc.; mutilation of the body, such as castration, vasectomy, tubal ligation, hysterectomy (without sufficient medical cause); immoral scientific research and its applications; bad example or scandal; disrespect for the dying or the dead; not trying to avoid war; showing aversion or contempt for others; refusing to speak to them when addressed; ignoring offers of reconciliation especially between relatives; cherishing an unforgiving spirit; raillery and ridicule; insults; irritating words and actions; sadness at another's prosperity; rejoicing over another's misfortune; envy at attention shown to others; tyrannical behavior; inducing others to sin by word or example; injury to health by over-indulgence; giving drink to others knowing they will abuse it; taking contraceptive pills which may or may not be an abortifacient; use of prophylactic or barrier methods to avoid pregnancy; using licit means of avoiding conception while fostering a contraceptive mentality; direct sterilization; causing unnecessary suffering or death to animals.

Sixth Commandment:
Thou Shalt Not Commit Adultery

Sins against the Sixth
Commandment are the following:

Impurity and immodesty in words, looks, and actions, whether alone or with others, telling and listening to dirty jokes; wearing immodest clothing; buying, renting or watching indecent movies, television or books (pornography as well as books which contain impurity); masturbation; fornication (sometimes called premarital sex); prostitution; sodomy (homosexual practices); adultery; divorce; polygamy; incest; sexual abuse; rape; prolonged and sensual kissing; petting or foreplay outside the context of marriage and within the context of marriage not ordering foreplay to the consummation of the natural conjugal act; immodest dancing; dating without taking the necessary precautions to safeguard purity or one's faith.

Seventh Commandment: Thou Shalt Not Steal

Sins against the Seventh Commandment are:

Stealing; petty thefts (e.g. taking things from one's place of employment to which one is not entitled or taking money from a family member without his permission); cheating; plagiarizing; breaking copyright regulations, (e.g. photocopying without permission); keeping borrowed or lost objects without making a reasonable attempt to restore the other's property; possession of ill-gotten goods; counseling or commanding someone to do injury to another person or to his goods; careless or malicious injury to the property of others; concealment of fraud, theft or damage when in duty bound to give the information; tax evasion by not paying just taxes; business fraud; dishonesty in politics, business, etc.; not paying just debts at scheduled time and neglecting to make reasonable efforts and sacrifices in this matter, e.g. by gradually laying up the amount required; not making reparation or compensation to someone suffering from unjust damages; forcing up prices by taking advantage of the ignorance or hardship of another; usury (lending money at high interest rates to someone in financial difficulty); speculation in which one contrives to manipulate the price of goods artificially in order to gain an advantage to the detriment of others; corruption in which one influences the judgment of those who must decide in legal matters; accepting bribes; appropriation and use for private purposes of the common goods of an enterprise; work poorly done; paying unjust wages or defrauding an employee of due benefits; forgery of checks and invoices; bouncing checks knowing that there is not enough funds to cover them; excessive expenses and waste; not keeping promises or contract agreements (if the commitments were morally just); gambling and betting (if they deprive someone of basic living needs for himself or others); excessive unnecessary waste of goods, resources, money or funds.

Eighth Commandment: Thou Shalt Not Bear False Witness against Thy Neighbor

Sins contrary to the Eighth Commandment:

Lying; boasting; bragging; flattery; hypocrisy; exaggerating; irony; sarcasm; unjust injury to another's good name either by revealing true and hidden faults (detraction); telling false defects (slander or calumny), tale-bearing, or spreading rumors; to criticize others, to listen with pleasure to others being criticized; gossiping; unjustly dishonoring another person in his presence (contumely); rash judgment (firmly believing, without sufficient reason, that someone has some moral defect); revealing secrets; publishing discreditable secrets about others, even if true; refusing or delaying to restore the good name one has blackened; baseless accusations; groundless suspicions; rash judgments of others in our own mind.

Ninth Commandment: Thou Shalt Not Covet Thy Neighbor's Wife

The Ninth Commandment forbids all those impure thoughts and desires which we take deliberate pleasure in so thinking, or we willingly consent to it whenever these unchaste thoughts or passions come into our mind. The penitent should keep in mind that any sin listed under the sixth commandment in which one willing or deliberately entertains may have the same degree of gravity, i.e. either mortal or venial sin.

Tenth Commandment: Thou Shalt Not Covet Thy Neighbor's Goods

The Tenth Commandment forbids the following:

Envy (desire for another's goods); jealousy (a zealous vigilance in keeping a good enjoyed by oneself from others); greed and the desire to have material goods without limit (avarice); the desire to become rich at all costs; businesses or professions who hope for unfavorable circumstances for others so that they may personally profit from it; envious of someone else's success, talents, temporal or spiritual goods; the desire to commit injustice by harming someone in order to get his temporal goods.

The Precepts of the Church

Besides the Ten Commandments of God, the faithful are also bound to follow the Precepts of the Church. The power for making these laws comes from Jesus Christ, and includes everything necessary for the government of the Church and for the direction of the faithful in order that they may attain their eternal salvation.

First Precept: To Assist at Holy Mass on All Sundays and Holy Days of Obligation

There are Six Holy days of obligation: 1. Christmas Day (December 25); 2. Mary, Mother of God (January 1); 3. Ascension Thursday (40 days after Easter); 4. The Assumption (August 15); 5. All Saints Day (November 1); 6. The Immaculate Conception (December 8).

The Church obliges us to abstain from servile work on Holy Days of Obligation, just as on Sundays, as far as we are able. Catholics who must work on Holy Days are obliged to attend Holy Mass unless excused by a reasonable grave cause. One may violate this precept by not attending Mass on the prescribed days or by arriving late to Mass without sufficient reason.

Second Precept: To Fast, Abstain, and Do Penance on Prescribed Days

The law of abstinence binds those who have completed their fourteenth year. The law of fasting binds those who have attained their age of majority (eighteen), until the beginning of their sixtieth year. Fasting means to eat less food than one normally eats.

On days of fasting, we are allowed only one full meal and two smaller meals together are less than one full meal; days of fasting are Ash Wednesday and Good Friday.

On days of abstinence, we are forbidden to eat flesh-meat; days of abstinence are: all of the Fridays of the year. In the United States, some form of penance or prayers may be done in place of the abstinence for those Fridays of the year outside of Lent. The permitted substitute penance could be: saying a Rosary, Stations of the Cross, visiting the sick or imprisoned, etc.

Third Precept: To Confess Our Mortal Sins at Least Once a Year

The Church urges us to go to the great Sacrament of Confession frequently, but only actually commands us to go at least once a year in order to warn those people who may have presumption on the mercy of God, which is a sin against the Holy Ghost. Parents must prepare their children for Confession when the children learn to distinguish right from wrong. (i.e. at about seven years of age). The obligation to confess once a year is only binding on those who have committed a mortal sin and have not confessed for at least one year.

Fourth Precept: To Receive Holy Communion during Easter Season

The Easter Season begins on the First Sunday of Lent and ends on Trinity Sunday. However, after receiving our First Holy Communion, it is strongly recommended to receive this great

Sacrament frequently during our lifetime (everyday if possible as recommended by Pope St. Pius X).

Fifth Precept: Contribute to the Support of the Church

This precept requires each to provide for the material needs of the Church according to his means.

Sixth Precept: To Observe the Laws of the Church Concerning Marriage.

Have I entered into marriage or aided anyone else to do so without permission from the Church to marry, or before a state official or a Protestant minister; or without dispensation within the forbidden degrees of kindred; or with any other known impediment?

APPENDIX F

Short Biographies
of the Saints Quoted

St. Aloysius Gonzaga
1568–1591

The privileged son of Marquis Ferrant Gonzaga and his wife Marta, St. Aloysius Gonzaga nonetheless perceived his life among society's elite to be meaningless. He answered the call of God to spend the rest of his life in the newly formed Jesuit order. He denounced his birthright and, in 1585, entered seminary with the purpose of filling his days with prayer, contemplation, and study.

In late 1591, the streets of Rome were littered with the dead and dying victims of the plague. Without concern for his own personal safety, St. Aloysius left the seminary to care for those who were ill. He contracted the disease in his ministrations to the plague victims. St. Aloysius died at the age of 23, having sacrificed his life for the care of others.

St. Alphonsus Liguori
1696–1787

In 1732, St. Alphonsus founded the Redemptorists (Congregation of the Most Holy Redeemer) and also an associated women's order. The apostolate of both was a common calling to live as Christ, in humility, serving the needy and the sick in testament to the mercy of Christ, the Redeemer. St. Alphonsus was made bishop thirty years later, although he initially resisted the appointment due to age and declining health. He wrote extensively on Marian theology and Eucharistic piety, which were the core of his personal spirituality. His famous works include *Marian Devotion*, *Prayers to the Divine Mother*, and *Visitations to the Blessed Sacrament*.

St. Ambrose
c. 340–397

Legend has it that bees covered the face of St. Ambrose as an infant, leaving a golden drop of honey on his lips. His parents took this as a sign that their child would grow to be a gifted speaker. Indeed, St. Ambrose developed a "honeyed tongue," which he exercised in politics. In 372, he became a governor of the provinces in northern Italy. He was so popular that in 374, he was acclaimed popularly as the bishop of Milan, even though he had not yet been baptized. He fled in horror upon hearing the news, but within a week he was baptized, ordained a priest, and consecrated as a bishop.

Upon this sudden entry into religious life, he assumed an ascetical lifestyle and gave away his wealth to the poor. As bishop, St. Ambrose exhibited a keen theological mind. He penned *De Sacramentis* (On the Nature of the Sacraments) and *De Spiritu Sancto* (On the Nature of the Holy Spirit), as well as hymns and other theological works. In 386, St. Ambrose baptized St. Augustine. St. Ambrose is a Doctor of the Church.

Blessed Angela of Foligno
c. 1248–1309

Blessed Angela of Foligno neglected her husband and family in order to seek out worldly pleasures. Rumors circulated about numerous affairs. Later in life, she termed this thirty-year period as "mortally sinful."

One day, after receiving the Eucharist unworthily, Blessed Angela of Foligno remorsefully cried out to Heaven. Afterward St. Francis appeared to her in a vision, urging her to confess her sins to the priest. Blessed Angela of Foligno was converted, and eventually she became a Third Order Franciscan. In reparation for her previous sins, she engaged in extreme penances and devoted herself to prayer. Following the deaths of her husband and children, she founded a women's religious community of Third Order Franciscans. With the help of her confessor, Blessed Angela of Foligno completed an account of her conversion and subsequent mystical visions titled, *Book of Visions and Instructions*. She bore visible stigmata at the conclusion of her life. Her remains are incorrupt in the Church of St. Francis, Foligno, Italy.

St. Anselm of Canterbury
1033–1109

St. Anselm of Canterbury determined at age 15 that his destiny was to be found in the Church. After initial resistance from his father, in 1060 St. Anselm tested his religious vocation with the Benedictine Community at the Abbey of Bec in Normandy. Only three years later, St. Anselm became prior there, and in 1079, he was consecrated as abbot. In 1070, after the death of Archbishop La Franc in Canterbury, St. Anselm reluctantly agreed to take Le Franc's place, although King William II was far from conciliatory. It is no surprise, in light of this fact, that St. Anselm fell into conflict with King William II of England.

In 1097, when St. Anselm returned to Rome on Church business, King William II seized Church property and did not allow St. Anselm to return to Canterbury. The successor to the throne, King Henry I, allowed St. Anselm back to Canterbury, although disputes led to a second exile from 1105–1107. After compromise was reached, St. Anselm finally returned to Canterbury to live out the rest of his years as archbishop. St. Anselm, besides being a prolific writer, helped to establish a vision of the Church with one internal authority, the pope of Rome; defended clerical celibacy; and developed the theological concept of the satisfaction theory of atonement.

St. Augustine of Hippo
354–430

Through the diligent prayers of his mother, St. Monica, St. Augustine of Hippo converted from a life of debauchery and drunkenness to become one of the most influential theologians and writers of the early Church. While at school in Carthage, he gained a reputation as an outstanding scholar. It was during this period, however, that he committed great immorality, ultimately taking a mistress with whom he fathered a child. After a series of teaching positions, he moved to Rome where his dramatic conversion took place in 383. After reading an account of St. Anthony of the Desert, which convicted him of his sinfulness, St. Augustine received an inner locution that directed him to "*tolle, lege*" (take up and read). St. Augustine found a Bible in a neighboring home, and his eyes fell upon the Epistle to the Romans, which he read in its entirety. He immediately embraced the Christian faith that he had forsaken and abandoned everything to become a monk and then a priest.

After a time, he was appointed bishop of Hippo, and he vigorously opposed the heresy of Pelagianism. His works, *Confessions* and *The City of God*, remain Christian classics today. He is a Doctor of the Church.

St. Basil the Great
c. 329–379

After his return from studies in Constantinople to practice law in Caesarea, St. Basil the Great underwent a radical spiritual conversion. He repented of a decadent lifestyle, was baptized, and then was appointed lector for the Church in Caesarea. Since he wanted to walk in the way of spiritual perfection, he searched out and visited monasteries in Egypt, Mesopotamia, Palestine, and Syria. Impressed by the humble and pious living of the monks, St. Basil the Great decided to become a monk himself and founded a monastery in Pontus. In due course, he composed a Rule for living in community. As the number of aspirants to the monastic life grew, St. Basil founded several other monasteries. Eventually, St. Basil was ordained in 370 and became the bishop of Caesarea. He retained this position until his death. His writings supported the Nicene Creed and the orthodoxy of Church doctrine over and against the heresy of Arianism. St. Basil the Great is a Doctor of the Church.

St. Benedict and St. Scholastica
c. 480–547

As a young man, St. Benedict left home searching for solitude. During his journey, he met a monk, Romanus of Subiaco, whose monastery was located above the cave in which St. Benedict took shelter. Romanus provided St. Benedict with the habit of a monk and there, for three years, St. Benedict remained, growing in the spiritual life as a hermit. In fact, St. Benedict's reputation for piety was such that after the death of a neighboring abbot, the monks pleaded with him to become the leader of their monastery. Sadly, jealousy over his election as abbot led some monks to poison St. Benedict. He was miraculously saved from their attempts.

He left the monastery and retreated back to his cave, both for safety and to return to a life of solitude. So many were attracted to his simplicity of life that St. Benedict eventually built a number of monasteries. One of St. Benedict's greatest accomplishments was the establishment of a written rule for monastic life in the West. For this reason he is called the "Father of the Western Monastic Movement."

At a very young age, St. Scholastica, the twin sister of St. Benedict, dedicated her life to God as a virgin. Later she went on to establish a religious community of women in Plombariola, Italy. She used her brother's Rule within the cloister in which she was appointed abbess. On the day St. Scholastica died, St. Benedict had a vision of her being received into the joys of Heaven.

St. Bernadette Soubirous
1844–1879

While gathering firewood at the grotto of Massabielle near Lourdes, France, St. Bernadette Soubirous saw a vision of a beautiful lady dressed in white with a blue girdle. Her companions were not witnesses to this apparition, but Bernadette reported that the Lady had asked her to return to the grotto every day for 15 days. Of course the news of St. Bernadette's encounter with the Lady spread like wildfire through the village. Crowds of people began to follow St. Bernadette to the grotto.

During the course of the visions, the Lady told Bernadette that priests should build a chapel at the site of the apparitions and organize processions there. During the ninth apparition, the Lady directed St. Bernadette to drink from the spring and to eat the wild plants. She dug at the earth but no spring was evident. Only days later did water gush forth. These very springs have since become a place of healing and solace to the suffering. During the last apparition, the Lady revealed that she was the "Immaculate Conception"; St. Bernadette had seen and conversed with the Blessed Virgin Mary.

Because of the attention focused upon St. Bernadette, she chose to leave Lourdes. First she went to a hospice school, an apostolate of the Sisters of Charity and Christian Instruction. Eventually St. Bernadette sought the life of a religious and entered the motherhouse at Nevers. Humbly, she ministered to the sick and dying in the infirmary. St. Bernadette was diagnosed with tuberculosis of the knee and died of the disease at the age of 35. Her body is incorrupt.

St. Bernard of Clairvaux
1090–1153

In his early twenties, St. Bernard, along with thirty companions, asked to be received into the Cistercian Order at Citeaux, known for its strict observance of the monastic rule. After his year as a novice, he made his profession and then was sent to the Abbey of Clairvaux. Due to his reputation as a natural leader, as well as his advanced knowledge of spirituality, St. Bernard of Clairvaux immediately was elevated to abbot of this new monastery. With this position, and in obedience to his superiors, St. Bernard of Clairvaux was thrust into a series of political and religious disputes, the most famous of which occurred in 1130 when he was appointed judge between Innocent II and Anacletus II, who both claimed to be the rightful pope of the Catholic Church (St. Bernard ruled in favor of Innocent II). As a man of tremendous wisdom, humility, and personal piety, St. Bernard was especially devoted to the Blessed Virgin Mary. St. Bernard wrote extensively on theological issues and produced Biblical commentary. He is a Doctor of the Church.

St. Bonaventure
1221–1274

St. Bonaventure took the Franciscan habit at age 22 and soon distinguished himself as an outstanding scholar at the University of Paris, where he became close friends with St. Thomas Aquinas. There he was awarded an advanced degree in theology in 1257. Such was his reputation for piety, leadership, and academics that in quick order he became the general of the Franciscans at age 35. Although never consecrated, St. Bonaventure served as archbishop of York for almost a year before being elevated to cardinal and bishop of Albano. He contributed much to the Franciscan Order, standardizing practices and writing the authoritative biography of St. Francis. He also wrote the multivolume work, *Commentary on the Sentences of Peter Lombard*, as well as other treatises that systemized theological thought. St. Bonaventure was a mystic who experienced ecstatic prayer as well as visions. His work *Journey of the Mind into God* reveals his intense spiritual life. He is a Doctor of the Church.

St. Catherine of Genoa
1447–1510

From early childhood, St. Catherine of Genoa had a deeply intimate relationship with God. As a young person, she devoted herself to the suffering Christ, taking on penances for the sins of the world. At 13, St. Catherine tried to enter a monastery but was turned away due to her young age. When she turned 16, in accordance with her parents' wishes, she was married to strengthen her family's political alliances. Unfortunately, her husband turned out to be a violent man whose erratic bouts of rage, as well as infidelity, brought constant strain to the marriage. Catherine endured his abusive behavior in silence, praying unceasingly for her husband's soul. Finally, through St. Catherine's intercession and enduring patience, her husband was converted and repented of his ways. After her husband's death, St. Catherine continued her work with the sick in the hospital of Genoa. Upon the order of her spiritual director, St. Catherine recorded her life's mystical experiences and spiritual insights from which the book *Memoirs of a Saint's Life* was eventually compiled.

St. Catherine of Siena
1347–1380

When she was only seven, St. Catherine of Siena began receiving visions and locutions from Christ and dedicated her virginity to Him. At age 16, she took the habit of the local Dominican Mantellates and freely cloistered herself within her own room at home. During this period, God infused her with deep spiritual knowledge, along with the grace of mystical union. St. Catherine of Siena left her solitary lifestyle in 1366 upon the order of Christ, rejoined her family, and set about the task of attending to those who were poor and suffering within her community. In 1370, she received a series of revelations on the natures of Hell, Purgatory, and Heaven. After the Dominican hierarchy examined and approved her religious beliefs, St. Catherine of Siena traveled throughout Italy advocating reform and repentance of the heart. One of her most famous journeys involved going to Avignon to convince Pope Gregory XI to return to Rome, which he did in 1377. St. Catherine of Siena wrote more than three hundred letters, many directly to the pope. *The Dialogue of Divine Providence* is her most famous work. She is a Doctor of the Church.

St. Clement I
Unknown–c. 100

Pope St. Clement I was a student of St. Peter and probably knew St. Paul. He wrote two letters that circulated in the early Church. One dealt with a dispute in Corinth in which St. Clement affirmed the priestly authority emanating from apostolic succession. The second one, attributed to his authorship, dealt with the virtues of a follower of Christ.

According to tradition, St. Clement was captured as a result of the persecution under Emperor Trajan and sent to work in a stone quarry. There he ministered among the Christians, offering comfort in this harsh environment. One day, he observed that fellow workers lacked sufficient water. St. Clement prayed and, upon opening his eyes, saw a lamb standing upon a hill, striking the ground with its hoof. He climbed to the site and, with his pickaxe, struck the earth. A stream of water came gushing forth. This event was the cause of many conversions among the pagans. In retribution, the Romans murdered St. Clement by drowning.

St. Cyprian
Unknown–258

After his Baptism in 245, St. Cyprian gave away a significant portion of his wealth to the destitute of Carthage and resigned his teaching position in order to dedicate his life to the Church. St. Cyprian was ordained a deacon shortly after his Baptism, was ordained a priest thereafter, and eventually was made bishop of Carthage by 249. During his episcopacy, St. Cyprian was involved in standardizing sacramental practices. In 256, during a wave of persecution under Emperor Valerian I, St. Cyprian publicly proclaimed Christ as Lord and Savior, steadfastly refusing to sacrifice to the emperor and the pagan deities. He was martyred for his bold witness to the Faith.

St. Dominic Savio
1842–1857

As a boy, St. Dominic Savio left his family to become a student at the Oratory founded by St. John Bosco in Turin, Italy. From the very beginning, St. Dominic Savio showed an extraordinary spiritual maturity. He would sit for hours in contemplation of Christ, adoring the Lord in the Blessed Sacrament or quietly praying by himself in the chapel. He was a sensitive soul, never wanting to offend God with even the tiniest venial sin. St. John Bosco encouraged his desire to enter the priesthood when he became older. Within the Oratory, St. Dominic Savio established a group known as the Company of the Immaculate Conception, which prayed for and assisted St. John Bosco with his nonpriestly duties. Recurrent lung problems caused St.

Dominic Savio to be sent home, where his condition worsened. He died on March 9, 1857, at only 15. St. John Bosco was so impressed with the example of St. Dominic Savio that he wrote a biography of the Saint's life.

Blessed Elizabeth of the Trinity
1880–1906

Despite an obstinate and fiery temper as a child, St. Elizabeth of the Trinity became a young adult with extraordinary compassion for God and others. She decided as a teenager to become a Discalced Carmelite but postponed entry until she was 21 due to her mother's objections. On August 2, 1901, St. Elizabeth's dream was fulfilled when she was received into the Dijon Carmel. Through letters, retreat notes, poems, and prayers, St. Elizabeth shared her profound insights into the mystery of the indwelling presence of the Holy Trinity. She died on November 9, 1906, after a period of extreme suffering from Addison's disease, then incurable.

St. Elizabeth Ann Seton
1774–1821

In 1794, newly married within the Anglican tradition, St. Elizabeth Ann Seton devoted herself to works of charity. A financial crisis within her husband's business, however, as well as his poor health, led the Setons to travel with their eldest daughter to Leghorn, Italy, to visit business associates. Sadly, her husband, William, died on December 27, 1803. While in Italy, St. Elizabeth

Ann Seton was introduced to the Catholic Church and there developed a deep love for the Mass.

After returning to America, on Ash Wednesday, March 14, 1805, St. Elizabeth Ann Seton was received into the Catholic Church. Her Protestant friends and family ostracized her and physical threats became commonplace. Finally, in conversation with Bishop Carroll, St. Elizabeth Ann Seton was invited to begin a school for the poor in proximity to St. Mary's Seminary in Emmitsburg, Maryland. St. Elizabeth Ann Seton took private vows and soon a religious community developed based on the Rule of the Sisters of Charity of St. Vincent de Paul. St. Elizabeth Ann Seton was elected Mother Superior of the Sisters of Charity (Emmitsburg) and served in that position until her death from pulmonary illness in 1821.

Ephrem the Syrian
c. 306–373

It is known that St. Ephrem lived an ascetical lifestyle as a religious. His writings reflected his community's deep felt commitment to offer one's entire existence to Christ. He composed biblical commentary, apologetics, and sermons critical of heresies prevalent during his day. Most notably, he defended the Church's teachings on the hypostatic union of Christ's two natures, human and divine, against the heresy of Docetism. In addition, St. Ephrem worked tirelessly to maintain the theological integrity between the Eastern and Western expressions of the Church. He was ordained a deacon and was present at the First Council of Nicaea. Even today, his hymnody and theological verse remain in use within the Eastern Churches.

St. (Mary) Faustina Kowalski
1905–1938

A vision of the suffering Christ invited St. Mary Faustina to leave the frivolities of the world and dedicate her life to Him as a religious. Eventually despite not having advanced education or a dowry, she was received into the Congregation of the Sisters of Mercy in Krakow. During her life with the sisters, St. Faustina experienced many mystical graces: visions, hidden stigmata, divine union, and the ability to read souls. But most of all, she perceived her calling as one who would, in cooperation with God, share His message of Divine Mercy for the salvation of souls. Jesus Christ gave St. Faustina the task of being His Apostle and "Secretary" of Divine Mercy to the world. Our Lord requested that His image of Divine Mercy, given to St. Faustina through a vision, be painted for veneration with the inscription "Jesus I Trust in You". Also, a new devotion, the Divine Mercy Chaplet, was to be prayed and the Feast of the Divine Mercy was established, as well as a prayer at the Hour of Mercy (3 p.m.) every day. St. Faustina recorded within her diary her reflections on Divine Mercy and all her mystical encounters with Christ. St. Faustina endured much suffering from tuberculosis toward the last years of her life, which she offered to God for the sake of sinners. She died at the age of 33.

St. Francis of Assisi
c. 1181–1226

St. Francis, in his youth, had little time for religion, preferring instead a good time at the local tavern with friends. In his early twenties, St. Francis set off to begin what he thought would be a military career but was taken captive for a year in Perugia, where he became seriously ill. On a second attempt, another illness prevented him from fighting. During his recuperation, he realized his life was empty of meaning. This proved to be a religious awakening. St. Francis returned to Assisi, on fire with the love of God.

One day, as St. Francis was praying before a crucifix in the run-down chapel of San Damiano, he heard the voice of Christ instructing him to rebuild His House that had fallen into ruin. St. Francis took the command literally, selling much of the fabric in his father's store for cash to rebuild the chapel. His father was furious and demanded that St. Francis be stripped of his inheritance. Before the bishop, St. Francis removed all his clothing and declared God to be his only Father. As St. Francis embraced "Lady Poverty," he preached the repentance of sins and displayed a gentle love toward all. As his followers grew in numbers, St. Francis journeyed to Rome to seek the approval of the Holy See for this newly formed religious society, the Friars Minor, and its rule of life that required absolute poverty, chastity, and obedience. Innocent III gave his official sanction to the group and the "Franciscan Order" was born. St. Francis received the stigmata in 1224 and was the recipient of visions, heavenly dreams, locutions, as well as miracles but remained a humble leader of the Friars Minor.

St. Francis de Sales
1567–1622

At the age of 12, St. Francis de Sales, while at the College de Clermont in Paris, was thrown into a spiritual crisis regarding the state of his immortal soul and the possibility of damnation. Although he excelled at his studies, he became very ill during this internal struggle and was sent home. At the Church of St. Etienne, the spiritual crisis miraculously subsided and he experienced God's loving presence flooding his soul. He transferred to the University of Padua to complete his education in law and theology. It was there that he decided to pursue a religious vocation. The bishop of Geneva arranged for St. Francis de Sales to be ordained and to serve as provost of the Cathedral Chapter in Geneva in 1593. Large numbers of Calvinists returned to the Church as a result of his evangelical preaching. In 1602, St. Frances de Sales was appointed bishop of Geneva. His works include *Introduction to the Devout Life* and *Treatise on the Love of God.* He also helped to found the Visitation Sisters in 1610 with St. Jane Frances de Chantal. He is a Doctor of the Church.

Servant of God, Bishop Fulton J. Sheen
1895–1979

Fulton Sheen attended St. Viator College in Bourbonnais, Illinois, before completing his theological education for the priesthood in St. Paul, Minnesota. After being ordained in 1919, he continued his academic work at Catholic University in Washington, DC, and at the University of Louvain in Belgium, where he completed his doctorate with honors. Bishop Sheen's early ministry was that of a lecturer of theology and philosophy in Catholic universities, both in Europe and in the United States, before being appointed auxiliary bishop of the Archdiocese of New York. He kept a very simple lifestyle, preferring to give away his earnings to the poor.

Bishop Sheen began his broadcast ministry in 1930 as a radio host for the Catholic Hour. As television developed into a viable communications medium, he appeared on Television Chapel, a local New York show. In 1952, Bishop Fulton Sheen attempted prime time national television. The show had a simple format: Bishop Sheen taught the basics of Christianity in a way to reach both Catholics and Protestants, along with his observations on culture and politics. The show was a hit and in 1952, he won an Emmy. The show, "Life Is Worth Living," aired through the fifties and sixties and is reairing today on religious stations. In 1966, Fulton was appointed archbishop of Rochester, New York. He served in this capacity until his retirement in 1969. He died from heart disease in 1979.

St. Gemma Galgani
1878–1903

By the age of 18, St. Gemma Galgani, following the deaths of her parents, assumed the primary responsibility of raising her younger siblings. Eventually when her family duties had been completed, St. Gemma received two marriage proposals, both of which she turned down to apply to the Passionist Monastery. She was rejected, however, due to ill health and the mystical experiences she reported having. Upon her return home, St. Gemma fell ill with meningitis. A miraculous cure came through the intercession of the Passionist, St. Gabriel Possenti, to whom St. Gemma prayed. She regularly experienced visions, inner locutions, ecstasy, foreknowledge of future events, and conversations with her Guardian Angel. On June 8, 1899, St. Gemma Galgani received the stigmata. This continued until the last three years of her life. The Giannini family, with whom she lived, recorded her words during ecstasies. St. Gemma Galgani died of tuberculosis at the age of 25.

St. Gabriel of Our Lady of Sorrows
1838–1862

St. Gabriel of Our Lady of Sorrows, after a series of family tragedies and misfortunes, gave up a career in the government to enter the Passionist monastery at Morrovalle, Italy. In doing so, he fulfilled promises made during personal illness that he would enter religious life upon recovery. An inner locution received during the procession of a venerated icon of the Blessed Virgin Mary urged him toward this goal in spite of his father's disapproval. A year after his entrance, St. Gabriel took his vows and was sent to the Monastery of Isola Gran Sasso. He excelled in his studies in preparation for ordination; however, he was diagnosed with tuberculosis and died prior to this dream being realized. Fellow monks acclaimed St. Gabriel of Our Lady of Sorrows for his holiness and perfect obedience to the Rule. Of his writings, only his letters and *Resolutions*, a spiritual work, are left.

St. Gertrude of Helfta
1256–c. 1302

St. Gertrude was born January 6, 1256, in Eisleben, Thuringia. It is thought that she was an orphan given into the care of the nuns of a Benedictine monastery in Helfta. She was an ardent student of literature and philosophy, but after a conversion to a more contemplative life as a nun, she became a highly influential mystic. Her most famous writing was the *Herald of God's Loving-Kindness.* Her visions of the heart of Jesus became part of the devotion to the Sacred Heart, popular in the Church ever since.

Pope St. Gregory I
c. 540–March 12, 604

In 574, St. Gregory I left a governmental post in Rome to become a monk. His ancestral home was converted into a monastery, and spiritual discipline filled his days. Only five years later, Pope Pelagius II called him out of his monastic enclosure to ordain him a deacon of Rome. He was sent to Byzantium to obtain help from Emperor Tiberius against the Lombards. Circa 586, St. Gregory I was recalled to Rome and was able, once again, to return to the monastery. Immediately, he was elected abbot by the community. In February 590, Pelagius II died and the clergy and people of Rome unanimously proclaimed St. Gregory I as the next pope. St. Gregory I was appalled. He tried to escape from the city but was captured and forcibly taken to the Basilica of St. Peter where he was consecrated as pope. Although plagued by ill health during his 14-year tenure as pope, St. Gregory I published numerous works, among them the famous *Regulae*

Pastoralis Liber that considers the role of the pastor as the physician of souls. He reformed the Roman liturgy, dealt with volatile political situations, and oversaw the dioceses of Italy. In his last years, St. Gregory's body was racked with unceasing pain. St. Gregory the Great is a Doctor of the Church.

Gregory of Narek
951–1003

Due to his mother's death and his father's position as an archbishop in the Armenian Rite, the responsibility for St. Gregory of Narek's education fell to a cousin, Anania of Narek, who was the founder of both a monastery and an accompanying school in Narek, Turkey. St. Gregory of Narek thrived there and ultimately decided to become an Armenian monk at the monastery. Within its walls, St. Gregory of Narek taught religion, composed poetry, and wrote commentary on Scripture. His mystical works revolved around the notion that one's sole purpose in life is the attainment of God: to unite one's nature, having reached a state of sanctification, to the Divine Nature of God (*theosis*). A collection of 95 prayers written by the Saint remains a cherished treasure within the Armenian culture. Many miracles have been attributed to St. Gregory of Narek, thus earning him the title "The Watchful Angel in Human Form."

St. Gregory of Nazianzus
c. 325–c.389

As a young priest ordained circa 328, St. Gregory of Nazianzus (also spelled Nazianzen) spoke out against the heresy of Arianism and strongly defended the Christian faith against the apostasy of Emperor Julian. St. Gregory's spiritual writings were some of the first to describe the process of *theosis* (sanctification) and mystical union with God. He was ordained bishop of Sasima by St. Basil in 372. His theological treatises on the nature of the Triune God, as found in the Nicene Creed, greatly influenced debate in Constantinople on Trinitarian doctrine. He is a Doctor of the Church.

St. Jane Frances de Chantal
1572–1641

As a young widow, St. Jane Frances de Chantal divested herself of her wealth, desiring instead to live in simplicity under a private vow of celibacy. Her father-in-law demanded, however, that she and her four children live at his large estate. She continued to aid the poor and the sick while managing the household, but she felt God's call to do something more. In time, St. Jane Frances de Chantal met St. Frances de Sales, then bishop of Geneva, who became her spiritual director. He affirmed her call to consecrated life; and in spite of much opposition, St. Jane Frances de Chantal formed a new religious community. The Congregation of the Visitation of the Blessed Virgin Mary, which she founded, welcomed older women as well as women in poor health and stressed the hidden, inner virtues of humility, meekness, and charity, using the model of the Blessed Mother's visitation to Elizabeth.

St. John Bosco
1815–1888

At the age of nine, St. John Bosco had a dream of a man dressed in radiant white who showed him that he was called to minister to delinquent and neglected boys. It was this dream that propelled St. John Bosco to devote himself to this cause. St. John Bosco's first appointment as a priest, however, was as chaplain to a girl's boarding school in Turin. Ultimately, St. John Bosco expanded his ministry to the prisons and taught catechism to the boys who lived on the streets. These boys would become the initial members of the Oratory of St. Francis de Sales. The first homes for orphaned boys were established in 1846. Throughout his ministry, St. John Bosco stressed the individual worth of each young person in the sight of God. In 1859, the Society of St. Francis de Sales (Salesians) was founded by St. John Bosco to help wayward boys, and in 1871 he, along with Mary Mazzarello, founded "Daughters of Mary, Help of Christians" to aid neglected girls.

St. Ignatius of Antioch
c. 35–c. 108

Tradition has it that St. Ignatius of Antioch was one of the children blessed by Jesus during his earthly ministry. In the year 69, St. Peter himself made St. Ignatius the Bishop of Antioch. In his letters to various churches, written hurriedly on his way to execution, St. Ignatius of Antioch gave instruction to the persecuted Christians. He wrote about the roles of bishops, priests, and deacons; the nature of God; and the importance of the Eucharist. He also promoted a change from the practice of observing the Jewish Sabbath on Saturday to the "Lord's Day" (Sunday). St. Ignatius of Antioch was the first to use the term "Catholic" to describe the Church. Emperor Trajan had St. Ignatius of Antioch brought to Rome to face death by wild beasts because he would not renounce his faith and participate in pagan sacrifice. St. Ignatius of Antioch welcomed death as a "kindness" as it allowed him to be united with God in Heaven. This witness of faith gave great comfort to the first-century Christians.

St. Ignatius of Loyola
1491–556

St. Ignatius of Loyola took up arms as a young man to fight as a Spanish knight. In 1521, during his recuperation from serious wounds received in the battle of Pamploma, he read the religious text *De Vita Christi* by Ludolph of Saxony and experienced a conversion of heart. Upon recovery, he traveled to the monastery of Our Lady of Montserrat where he hung his military garb before the statue of the Virgin. During this time, he was graced with a vision of the Virgin holding her Son. Following academic study in Spain and France, St. Ignatius took solemn vows in 1534 to dedicate his life as a missionary to pagan lands, thus laying the foundation for a new religious order known as the Society of Jesus (Jesuits). St. Ignatius, as the first Superior General, guided the community in its apostolate of evangelism and oversaw the formation of Catholic schools throughout Europe. During the Protestant Reformation, St. Ignatius wrote in defense of the Catholic Faith. He was instrumental in composing the *Jesuit Constitution* that was adopted in 1540. *The Spiritual Exercises*, a masterpiece in spiritual guidance, remains a popular text in Christian spirituality. St. Ignatius died in Rome from malaria.

St. Irenaeus
c. 125–202

St. Irenaeus, a priest from Lyon, escaped the persecution by Emperor Marcus Aurelius because he had been sent to Rome to deliver reports on the heresy of Montanism. When he returned, St. Irenaeus was appointed the second bishop of Lyon, the first having been martyred. The Church, already beaten down by Roman tyranny, was further weakened by heretical teachings. As he sought to restore order and build up the body of Christ, St. Irenaeus wrote the multivolume work *Adversus Haereses*, which refuted Gnosticism. St. Irenaeus also wrote about the role of Mary in salvation history and her perpetual virginity as a necessary doctrine of belief. Throughout his writings, he supported the authenticity of all four gospels as canonized Scripture and the role of the bishop to offer accurate interpretation of the sacred texts. He is a Doctor of the Church.

St. Jerome
c. 342–420

After he completed his education, St. Jerome decided he wanted to explore other lands. In Gaul, he collected religious manuscripts, including those of St. Hilary, to bring back to Rome. In 373, he attempted another journey but fell ill in Antioch. During this illness, his heart opened to God, and he was filled with a burning desire to take up a penitential life and study Holy Scripture.

St. Jerome went to live in the desert near Antioch and learned Hebrew from one of the hermit monks. After a time, St. Jerome was called back to Rome and there was ordained to the priesthood. He assisted Pope Damasus by writing in defense of the perpetual virginity of the Blessed Virgin Mary, the discipline of celibacy for priests, and the veneration of Saints' relics. His greatest achievement, the one for which he is most famous, was his work on what would become the Vulgate Bible. He translated the majority of Old Testament text into Latin from the original Hebrew and revised the Latin New Testament according to the original Koine Greek, adding extensive commentary. St. Jerome also established a monastery in Bethlehem along with a women's community of religious. He is a Doctor of the Church.

Blessed Pope John XXIII
1881–1963

Blessed Pope John XXIII entered seminary in Bergamo in 1892. In 1896, he was admitted to the Secular Franciscans, making

religious profession on May 23, 1897. He continued his seminary studies at the Pontifical Seminary and was ordained a priest
in 1904. During WWI, he was drafted and served in the medical
corps and as a chaplain. After the war, he was appointed the
Italian president of the Society for the Propagation of the Faith,
and in 1925, Pope Pius XI selected him to be the apostolic visitor to Bulgaria. Later in 1935, he was made Apostolic Delegate
to Turkey and Greece. When World War II broke out, he used
his influence and office to save thousands of Jewish refugees in
collaboration with the underground resistance. After WWII, he
was appointed a cardinal. Through the guidance of the Holy
Spirit, on October 28, 1958, Blessed John XXIII was elected pope
after the death of Pius XII. Although his pontificate lasted only
five years, his pastoral approach and his initiation of the Second
Vatican Council forever made an indelible mark on the Church.

St. John Chrysostom
349–407

Around the year 375, St. John Chrysostom became a hermit,
living in poverty and isolation. He spent two years with little
sleep, stood throughout the day as a penance, and memorized
the Bible as an act of discipline. In the course of time, he came
to live in Antioch, where he was acclaimed for his deep personal
piety and love for God. In 381, he was ordained as a deacon
and in 386, St. John Chrysostom was ordained a priest. In 398,
against his wishes, he was elected archbishop of Constantinople. He greatly disapproved of the hedonism of the imperial
court there and spoke strongly against its moral laxity. Empress
Eudoxia, whom he condemned for her lavish lifestyle, became

very unhappy with this troublesome archbishop. Eventually, St. John Chrysostom was exiled to Armenia after he protested the placement of a silver statue of Eudoxia near the cathedral premises. He died on the journey. His last words were "Glory be to God for all things." He is a Doctor of the Church.

St. John Climacus
c. 525–606

At 16, St. John Climacus left his family and all his belongings to seek out a life of solitude and prayer. Having heard of the pious reputation of St. Catherine's Monastery, he traveled to Mt. Sinai, placing himself as a novice under the monk, Martyrius. After his spiritual director's death, St. John Climacus, desiring greater asceticism, lived alone for the next twenty years in a hermitage at the base of Mt. Sinai. There he engaged in intense prayer, penance, and study, while growing in holiness and wisdom. Eventually, the monks of St. Catherine's persuaded St. John Climacus, at the age of 75, to become the abbot of the community. St. John Climacus wrote a number of books on the spiritual life, among them, *The Ladder of Divine Ascent* (*Scala Klimax*), which describes the soul's journey to mystical union with God. St. John Climacus is a Doctor of the Church.

Blessed John Henry Cardinal Newman
1801–1890

In 1816, Blessed John Henry Newman, then an Anglican, became a student at Trinity College, Oxford. During this time, he was drawn to the Anglican priesthood. After continued study at Oriel College, Oxford, he was ordained a deacon in 1824 and a priest in 1825. Although he had defended Anglicanism as a *via media* ("middle way") between Roman Catholicism and Protestantism, Blessed John Henry Newman had serious doubts about the validity of the Anglican Church. In 1845, he formally recanted any negative statements he had made about the Church of Rome and became a Roman Catholic himself. In 1846, he became a priest and, while in Rome, joined the Community of Oratorians. Although never a bishop, he was made a cardinal on May 12, 1879. Blessed John Henry Newman was known for his superior intellect and vast collection of writings that include *The Dream of Gerontius*, *The Idea of a University*, and *Apologia Pro Vita Sua*.

St. John of the Cross
1542–591

On February 24, 1563, desiring to lead a life of prayer, St. John of the Cross entered the Carmelite Order. He was professed in 1564 and ordained in 1567. After a time, he found that he desired a more disciplined, solitary life than what prevailed in the Carmel of his day. He was considering a move to the stricter Carthusian Order until he met St. Teresa of Avila. A common spiritual understanding shared with St. Teresa influenced him to join the reform movement of Carmel. His superiors, however, met this decision with great hostility. He was imprisoned, brutally beaten, and starved. On August 15, 1578, he escaped through a window and fled for his life to a convent of the reform movement. In spite of such cruel treatment, St. John of the Cross boldly continued to assist St. Teresa of Avila, founding houses for what has become known as the Discalced Carmelite Order. Today he is revered by both branches of Carmelites (O. Carm; OCD). *The Spiritual Canticle,* based loosely on the Song of Songs, and *The Ascent of Mt. Carmel,* a spiritual study of the soul's journey to union with God, are among his most popular works. He is a Doctor of the Church.

Blessed John Ruysbroeck
1293–1381

After his ordination as a priest in 1317, Blessed John Ruysbroeck composed treatises in the vernacular condemning any practices of mysticism and teachings that were contrary to the Magisterium of the Catholic Church. The writings he produced caused such an uproar among the superstitious peasantry that he and his companions had to flee for their safety to the hermitage of Groenendael in Soignes. Eventually, so many men joined his cause for orthodox Catholic practice that a community of Canons Regular was established on March 13, 1349. Blessed John was elected prior of this new community and flourished as a writer. His most famous work, *The Spiritual Espousals,* deals with the contemplative life. Blessed John was beloved in the community for his gift of teaching and his saintly nature. He died at age 88.

St. John Vianney
1786–1859

Deemed lacking in "mental suppleness," St. John Vianney failed to pass the Latin requirement for entrance into the seminary at Verrieres, France. Although he succeeded on the second try, St. Vianney always was labeled as having slightly below average intelligence. No doubt, his sporadic education as a child as well as finding himself, through a series of coincidences, hiding for a time from forced conscription in Napoleon's army, were contributing factors that slowed his studies. When he finally completed his training, his superiors assigned him to a remote village. Soon it was apparent that this "Curé d'Ars" had an extraordinary depth of personal spirituality and was a man of great virtue. People from all over France flocked to Ars to seek spiritual advice, to receive the Sacrament of Reconciliation, and to listen to his teaching. St. Vianney would spend 16 to 18 hours a day in the confessional. He loved his people wholeheartedly and offered prayers and penances for their welfare. He is upheld as the model for parish priests.

Blessed Jordan of Saxony
c. 1190–1237

After hearing the renowned preaching of Blessed Reginald of Orleans in 1220, Blessed Jordan of Saxony decided to leave his studies at the University of Paris and enter the Order of Preachers (Dominicans). Blessed Jordan of Saxony loved the Rule of St. Dominic and quickly rose to leadership positions in the order. He became the first provincial of the Lombardy province and later succeeded St. Dominic as Master General of the Order upon St. Dominic's death. Blessed Jordan of Saxony was well known as a compelling preacher, gaining over a thousand new vocations during his university lecture tours. He also authored *Libellus de Principiis Ordinis Praedicatorum* (*Booklet on the*

Beginnings of the Order of Preachers), in which he offered the first biography of St. Dominic as well as a history of the order itself. Blessed Jordan died in a shipwreck while returning from a visitation of Dominican priories in Palestine.

St. Josemaría Escrivá
1902–1975

A turning point in the spiritual development of St. Josemaría Escrivá came during Christmastide 1917 in his hometown of Barbastro, Spain. He looked out the window of his home and saw the footprints of a Discalced Carmelite in the snow. As he pondered the Carmelite's sacrifice of not wearing shoes in the frigid cold, St. Josemaría Escrivá realized that he, too, wanted to offer himself up totally to God. At that very point, he resolved to become a priest. He was ordained shortly after his father's death on March 28, 1927. In October 1928, God gave St. Josemaría Escrivá a vision of founding a religious community composed of secular laypeople who would dedicate themselves to God's will, promising a radical, personal commitment to love Christ and neighbor within everyday life. This became Opus Dei. St. Josemaría Escrivá left an abundance of books on workplace spirituality, films, as well as recorded talks of his preaching missions.

St. Lawrence of Brindisi
1559–1619

St. Lawrence of Brindisi was a member of the Capuchin Order in Verona. Known to be a brilliant scholar, St. Lawrence of

Brinsdisi was ordained, and in 1596 he was appointed to a post in Rome. At first his ministry focused on the conversion of the Jewish people in Italy. After a time, he was sent to Germany to combat the rise of Lutheranism. In 1601, at the command of Emperor Rudolf III, he assisted in forming an army of Germans to hold off the Turks who were threatening an attack on Hungary. St. Lawrence became this army's chaplain and was instrumental in securing victory over the Muslim forces. Yet, in the midst of all this activity, St. Lawrence composed a massive number of homilies and Scripture commentaries, as well as establishing friaries. His celebration of the Mass was often marked by ecstasy, and he promoted devotion to the rosary and Marian prayer. St. Lawrence is considered one of the greatest contemplatives of the Catholic Church. He is a Doctor of the Church.

Pope St. Leo the Great
c. 400–461

Pope St. Leo the Great chose to abandon a life of riches in order to enter religious life. While a deacon, he was sent to Gaul to arbitrate a number of political disputes. Upon his return, he found that he had been elected unanimously as pope after the death of Pope Sixtus III. During his pontificate, the papacy became the centralized authority on spiritual and temporal matters for the Church. By means of the good relationship Pope St. Leo the Great had established with Emperor Valentinian III, an imperial decree was issued on June 6, 445, affirming the primacy of the bishop of Rome. The hierarchy of the Church, with the pope as its head, took visible form through his efforts. He used his power to defend Rome against the invasion of Attila the Hun in the fifth century. In addition, he wrote extensively on Church doctrine. Pope St. Leo the Great is a Doctor of the Church.

Blessed Louis and Blessed Zelie Martin
Louis: 1823–1894
Zelie: 1831–1877

As a young man, Blessed Louis Martin desired to serve God as a Carthusian priest. Due to an inability to learn Latin, he soon abandoned this idea in order to begin work as a watchmaker and jeweler in Alençon, France. Blessed Zelie also wanted a religious vocation; however, a prioress convinced her that she was called to secular life. Blessed Zelie learned Alençon's famous lace stitching and soon was running her own business. One day, as Blessed Zelie passed Blessed Louis, she had an inner locution indicating that Blessed Louis was the one whom God had chosen for her husband. Not long after that, the two formally met and soon were married.

The home of Blessed Louis and Blessed Zelie centered on God and was a place of great love. Blessed Louis gave up watchmaking to supervise Zelie's lace business. In late 1876, Blessed Zelie found an inoperable cancerous growth on her breast. Sadly, she died less than a year later. Zelie had given birth to nine children, four of whom died in childhood. All the remaining children grew up to serve God in religious vocations as nuns. One child, Thérèse, was declared a Saint. Blessed Louis moved to Lisieux after Blessed Zelie's death in order to be close to relatives. The last years of his life were full of great suffering offered to God.

St. Thérèse described her parents as "parents without equal, worthy of heaven, holy ground permeated with the perfume of purity." It is a fitting tribute to the sanctity of both Blessed Zelie and Blessed Louis Martin.

St. Louis-Marie de Montfort
1673–1716

After his ordination in 1700, St. Louis de Montfort joined the Third Order Dominicans. Soon, he was appointed as hospital chaplain at Poitiers. Perceiving that he was called to a different kind of ministry, St. Louis de Monfort asked guidance from the Holy Father. Pope Clement XI appointed him Apostolic Missionary so that St. Louis de Montfort would be able to preach and conduct missions in France. The years that followed were extremely productive. He preached with a kind of supernatural power that moved listeners to profound remorse for their sins. In addition, he wrote a number of Marian treatises, *True Devotion to Mary* and *The Secret of Mary* being the most notable. He established a Rule for the Company of Mary and a religious society for women called the Daughters of Mary. His fiery preaching did make enemies among the Jansenists, who tried to kill him with poison in his dinner broth. Although an antidote was administered, he was plagued with ill health afterward. He died at the age of 43. Many healing miracles have been attributed to his intercession.

St. Martin of Tours
c. 315–c.400

St. Martin of Tours had an extraordinary spiritual encounter while a soldier. A beggar, in tatters and freezing from the cold, approached him at the city gates of Amiens. St. Martin of Tours, his heart full of compassion for the poor man, gave him half of his military cloak. The following night, St. Martin of Tours had a vision in which Jesus himself was the beggar wearing the cloak. This vision prompted him to seek Baptism right away. In the remainder of this military service, St. Martin of Tours refused to take up arms against the enemies of Rome. After his discharge, St. Martin of Tours went to Poitiers to become a monastic. Raising the dead to life again, supernaturally healing the sick, casting out demons, and performing other miracles were attributed to this saintly man. Eventually, St. Martin of Tours founded the Monastery of Ligug. Reluctantly, he left the monastery to become the bishop of Tours due to the insistence of the people. St. Martin died in his early eighties.

St. Mary Magdalen de Pazzi
1566–1607

Even from early childhood, St. Mary Magdalen de Pazzi was extolled as having great love for our Lord and for the practices of prayer and penance. She possessed an intense desire for the Eucharist. The sisters at her convent school were amazed at her spirituality and predicted Sainthood for this precocious student. In December 1582, St. Mary Magdalen de Pazzi entered the Carmelite convent of Santa Maria degli Angeli and was professed early due to a serious life-threatening illness. Miraculously St. Mary Magdalen recovered and during her lifetime received many ecstasies and spiritual gifts, among them the ability to read souls and bilocate. The Carmelite sisters recorded the spiritual conversations of St. Mary Magdalen while she was in ecstasy and published them as *Maxims of Divine Love.*

St. Maximus the Confessor
c. 580–662

Sometime around 614, St. Maximus the Confessor left his government appointment in Constantinople to take up monastic life at the Monastery of Philippicus, Turkey. Because of the invasion of forces from Persia, he fled to Carthage; it was there that he wrote the bulk of his theological works. *Mystagogy* focuses on the spiritual realities of the Eucharistic liturgy. He also swayed the Lateran Council of 649 to reject the Monothelite heresy (i.e., Christ did not have a human will). Unfortunately, Emperor Constans II had embraced this false teaching, and as a result of the political situation, St. Maximus the Confessor was convicted of heresy in 662. His tongue and right hand were cut off, and he was exiled. He died shortly afterward in 662. The Sixth Ecumenical Council vindicated St. Maximus the Confessor. He was declared a Doctor of the Church.

St. Paul Miki
1564–1597

St. Paul Miki became a Christian when his entire family converted to the Faith through the influence of Jesuit missionaries in Osaka, Japan. At twenty, St. Paul Miki entered the Jesuit Seminary at Azucki and was received as a member of the Society of Jesus only two years later. He was an eloquent speaker, noted for his powerful homilies that converted many Buddhists. In 1587, the political tide turned. The government perceived the popularity of Catholicism to be a threat and took stern measures to ban its practice, especially all overt forms of evangelism. Catholics, if caught, were to be put to death. St. Paul Miki was only a few months from ordination as a Catholic priest when he was discovered and arrested. After being forced on a month long march to Nagasaki, St. Paul Miki and other prisoners arrived at the place of execution. Faced with the sentence of death by crucifixion, he continued to proclaim the love of God, joining to sing a *Te Deum* as the executioners fastened the Christians to their crosses. With his last breath, St. Paul Miki forgave his persecutors. A secret community of Christians established in Nagasaki kept the memory of St. Paul Miki and his teachings alive for future generations.

St. Perpetua
181–203

St. Perpetua, a married noblewoman, was arrested during the persecution of the early Church under the Roman emperor, Septimius Serverus, in Carthage. Her pagan father exerted tremendous pressure upon St. Perpetua to renounce Christianity for the sake of the family's name and her young son. She and Felicity, her slave and an expectant mother herself, were condemned to death. *The Passion of St. Perpetua, St. Felicity, and their Companions*, records her visions prior to death. St. Perpetua showed remarkable courage and steadfast faith in the face of an agonizing death from wild beasts. She was a role model in the early Church.

St. Peter Damian
1007–1072

After being deemed a hardship upon his impoverished family, as an infant St. Peter Damian was left to starve by his mother. Only a servant's stern words, reminding his mother that this would be a mortal sin, spared his life. This kind of mistreatment was to continue even after his parents' deaths until another brother, an archpriest in Ravenna, took St. Peter Damian under his wing. Impressed with two religious from the Order of St. Benedict, St. Peter Damien ultimately joined the hermitage of Fonte Avellino and became a monk. In 1043, under obedience, he became prior of the monastery. Reluctantly he was drawn into the political intrigues within the Church. He strongly advocated disciplined living, and assigned penances for clergy and laity alike who did not strictly adhere to appropriate Christian behavior. He condemned simony, unfaithfulness to the vows of celibacy, and lax morals. St. Peter Damian is a Doctor of the Church.

St. (Padre) Pio of Pietrelcina
1887–1968

By the time St. Pio of Pietrelcina was five years old, he discerned the call of God to the religious life, taking the Blessed Virgin Mary as his model of perfect obedience. On January 22, 1903, at the age of 15, he received the Franciscan habit; five years later he made his solemn vows; and in 1910 he was ordained. Finally St. Pio of Pietrelcina, after several assignments that did not work out for health reasons, was assigned to the Capuchin Friary at San Giovanni Rotondo. With the exception of very brief military service, St. Pio remained at San Giovanni until he died. St. Pio of Pietrelcina exhibited extraordinary mystical gifts throughout his monastic life: He experienced bilocation, levitation, the ability to read souls, visions, the gift of languages, inner locutions, transverberation, and the visible stigmata. The Masses he celebrated attracted people from all over the world, and individuals waited for days to receive the Sacrament of Reconciliation from this holy priest. St. Pio of Pietrelcina often said later in life that his most joy-filled moment was the opening of the hospital, Casa Sollievo della Sofferenza, which he helped to create in San Giovanni Rotondo, and his greatest treasure, the Holy Sacrifice of the Mass.

St. Robert Bellarmine
1542–1621

St. Robert Bellarmine felt called to a religious vocation in the Society of Jesus, and in 1560 he entered the novitiate in Rome. His superiors sent him to Leuven (near Brussels) to complete his education. In 1576, St. Robert Bellarmine was appointed lecturer at the new Roman College. He remained at this post for 11 years, speaking and writing in defense of the Catholic Church and becoming a warrior in apologetics. His *Disputationes de Controversiis Christianae Fidei* (*Disputationes*) was the first work of its kind to offer a systematic defense of Catholic doctrine in light of controversies promulgated by Protestantism. He was assigned in 1592 to write the *Preface of the Latin Vulgate* by Pope Clement VIII. He then went on to become rector of the Roman College. Prior to his death, St. Robert devoted himself to spiritual matters, writing *The Mind's Ascent to God*, *The Art of Dying Well*, and *The Seven Words on the Cross*. St. Robert Bellarmine is a Doctor of the Church.

St. Robert Southwell
c. 1561–February 21, 1595

In 1578, St. Robert Southwell, a British subject, was received into the Society of Jesus (Jesuits) at Rome and ordained a priest in 1584. In that same year, Queen Elizabeth I, in order to promulgate the Church of England, enacted a law that forbade Catholic priests ordained after her accession to the throne to remain in England any more than forty days. Yet St. Robert Southwell was moved by the Spirit of God to return to England in 1586 as a Jesuit missionary, even though, if detected, it would mean a sure and certain death. After six years of secretly ministering to recusant Catholics, his activities were found out, and St. Robert was charged with treason against the Crown. He was hanged, drawn, and quartered. His last action was to try to make the Sign of the Cross, with his bound hands, while hanging from the gallows. His poems and letters, especially the publication *Marie Magdalen's Funeral Tears*, served to boost the morale of persecuted Catholics and remind them that the suffering of this world is minor when compared to the joys of Heaven.

St. Teresa of Avila
1515–1582

St. Teresa of Avila, the foundress of the Discalced Branch of Carmelites, entered the Carmel of the Incarnation near Avila, Spain. As a religious, she experienced bouts of illness as well as spiritual aridity. During 1559, and for several years following, Teresa had visions of Jesus Christ in which she entered into mystical union. During the same time period, St. Teresa became disillusioned with the lax observance of the Rule of St. Albert.

In 1563, with papal sanction, St. Teresa of Avila left Incarnation Monastery to found a Carmel whose members would be devoted more fully to prayer and austere practices. More Carmels eventually were established, many in Spain by St. Teresa of Avila herself, in accordance with the reform. She was a prolific writer. Pope Paul VI proclaimed St. Teresa of Avila a Doctor of the Church in 1970. Both the Discalced (OCD) and the Carmelites of the Ancient Observance (O. Carm.) today look to St. Teresa of Avila as a reformer and teacher of Carmel.

Blessed Teresa of Calcutta
1910–1997

Blessed Teresa of Calcutta left her homeland of Albania at age 18 to fulfill a call felt since childhood to become a missionary sister. Once professed in the Sisters of Loreto, she was assigned to Calcutta, India, and was very happy working at a convent school. Blessed Teresa of Calcutta's life changed dramatically on September 10, 1946, when, while traveling back to Calcutta from retreat in Darjeeling, Blessed Teresa heard "God's call within a call." God, through an inner locution, directed her to leave the convent and be poor among the poor, ministering to the needs of India's most impoverished people.

With the approval of Rome, on October 7, 1950, the Missionaries of Charity formally began as a diocesan congregation that would care for "the poorest of the poor." As the Mother Superior of the Missionaries of Charity, Blessed Teresa of Calcutta encountered tremendous hardship and criticism, as well as spiritual darkness and aridity. She was an outspoken critic of abortion and organized orphanages for the care of unwanted children, in addition to caring for the needs of the poor. Blessed Teresa of Calcutta received the Nobel Peace Prize for her work with the poor of the world.

St. Thérèse of Lisieux
1873–1897

After the loss of her mother, Zelie, to cancer, as well as her older sister, Pauline, to the cloistered life of Carmel, St. Thérèse of Lisieux came down with a mysterious illness characterized by serious fevers, tremors, and periods of delirium. This state lasted until May 13, 1883, when she experienced a miraculous healing after she observed a smiling face on a family statue of the Blessed Virgin Mary. On Christmas Eve 1886, St. Thérèse underwent a profound spiritual conversion, and from that point on, her goal was to enter Carmel, dedicating her life entirely to God. In May 1887 she pleaded her cause during a general audience with Pope Leo XIII. Although he was noncommittal about her entrance, it became a reality on April 9, 1888, when she was approved for early entrance.

From all outward appearances, St. Thérèse's time in Carmel was unremarkable; with the exception of a few sisters, no one realized the extraordinary depth of her hidden spiritual life. Under obedience to Pauline, Mother Agnes of Jesus, St. Thérèse wrote her spiritual autobiography, *The Story of a Soul.* After her death from tuberculosis, her writings revealed her vocation as Love in the heart of the Church, as well as her concept of "the little way of spiritual childhood," the path toward holiness that she had lived so fully in Carmel. Her deathbed conversations were recorded, and she leaves also a number of prayers, poems, and letters. St. Thérèse is a Doctor of the Church.

St. Thomas Aquinas
c. 1225–1274

After a childhood dedicated to academic study, particularly philosophy, St. Thomas Aquinas decided to join the Dominican Order at age 19. In 1245, he was sent to the University of Paris and while there met the Dominican scholar Albert the Great. When Magnus was appointed professor in Cologne's *Studium*

Generale, St. Thomas followed and was given the position of second lecturer and *magister studentium*. This was a significant turning point in his life, marking the start of his public teaching career and the beginning of his prolific writings on theology, ethics, and general philosophy, as well as other topics related to Church doctrine and worship practices. He traveled extensively between France and Italy during his lifetime, lecturing in the universities. He asserted that Truth is known through both reason and faith; he believed that all people can ascertain the Truth of God through the process of properly disposed human reasoning using natural revelation. His most noted work is the *Summa Theologica*, wherein he details proofs for the existence of God. St. Thomas is a Doctor of the Church.

St. Thomas More
February 7, 1478–July 6, 1535

St. Thomas More was a lawyer in Great Britain during the reign of King Henry VIII, where he gained a reputation for honesty and faithful service. The king noticed his work and appointed him first as counselor and personal servant and then as privy counselor in 1518. St. Thomas More became more entangled in politics when the king ordered him to serve as his own personal secretary and advisor. Soon after, upon Thomas Cardinal Wolsey's recommendation, St. Thomas More became the Speaker of the House of Commons in 1523. After Wolsey fell out of favor with the King, St. Thomas More was appointed in his stead as Lord Chancellor. As a devout Catholic, St. Thomas More incurred the wrath of the king when he refused to sign a letter requesting that the pope annul the marriage of King

Henry VIII to Catherine of Aragon. Moreover he noticeably was absent at the coronation of Anne Boleyn as the Queen of England. But what sealed his fate was his refusal to swear allegiance to the Act of Succession. For this he was tried for treason and found guilty. St. Thomas More was beheaded for defending the Catholic Church and the authority of the pope in religious matters. He wrote a number of treatises condemning the Protestant Reformation. Prior to his death, while imprisoned, he wrote *Comfort against Tribulation.*

About the Authors

Deacon Richard G. Ballard serves as pastoral associate at Our Lady of the Rosary Catholic Church in Greenville, South Carolina. A convert to the Church, Deacon Ballard served as a Lutheran parish pastor for almost 25 years before entering the Church in 2006. He was ordained a permanent deacon for the Diocese of Charleston in 2010. He completed his undergraduate studies in religion at Mars Hill College. He holds a Master of Divinity degree and doctorate in pastoral theology from Lutheran Theological Southern Seminary; Master's degree in counseling from the University of South Carolina; and Master of Sacred Theology degree from the Lutheran Theological Semiary at Gettysburg. He has completed postgraduate work in bereavement at Madonna University.

Ruth H. Ballard is a graduate of Old Dominion University, Norfolk, Virginia, and holds a master's degree in theology from Southeastern Baptist Theological Seminary. She completed additional graduate studies at the Lutheran Theological Southern Seminary. Prior to her conversion to the Catholic Faith, she served as a Lutheran parish pastor for over 18 years. Ruth writes (paints) icons and creates original contemporary artwork, including mosaics on religious themes, and lectures and teaches classes on the subject. She is a lay Carmelite. Her website is http://www.sacred creations.biz.

Ronda Chervin, PhD, is presently a professor of philosophy and spirituality at Holy Apostles College and Seminary in Cromwell, Connecticut. She is a grandmother and a dedicated widow. Dr. Chervin has taught at such Catholic institutions as Loyola Marymount University, the Seminary of Los Angeles, Franciscan University of Steubenville, Notre Dame Apostolic Institute, and Our Lady of Corpus Christi. She is the author of some sixty books about Catholic thought and life and is also a presenter on ETWN, FOCUS TV, and Relevant Radio. Look for her websites, http://www.rondachervin.com and http://www .spiritualityrunningwithgod.com, and for her blog, http://www .ccwatershed.com.